THE ACTOR UNCOVERED

A LIFE IN ACTING

Michael Howard

ALLWORTH PRESS
NEW YORK

Allworth Press books may be purchased in bulk at special discounts for sales promotion, corporate gifts, fund-raising, or educational purposes. Special editions can also be created to specifications. For details, contact the Special Sales Department, Allworth Press, 307 West 36th Street, 11th Floor, New York, NY 10018 or info@ skyhorsepublishing.com.

20 19 18 17 16 5 4 3 2 1

Published by Allworth Press, an imprint of Skyhorse Publishing, Inc.
307 West 36th Street, 11th Floor, New York, NY 10018.

Allworth Press® is a registered trademark of Skyhorse Publishing, Inc.®, a Delaware corporation.

www.allworth.com

Front cover photo credit Whitney Bauck

Library of Congress Cataloging-in-Publication Data is available on file.

Print ISBN: 978-1-62153-549-2
Ebook ISBN: 978-1-62153-558-4

Printed in the United States of America

This book is dedicated, as is the best of my life,
to my partner, my wife — the extraordinary Betty —
and to my sons, Matthew and Christopher.

"We take our work seriously, but not ourselves."
—Michael Howard

TABLE OF CONTENTS

III: IN PERFORMANCE

IV: THE CONTINUING PROFESSION

Introduction
By Michael Kahn

There is no one who has had a more lasting influence on my journey as a theater artist than the wise and generous Michael Howard, the author of this wise and generous book.

I first met Michael—"Mr. Howard" as he was then to me—at the beginning of my third year at the High School of Performing Arts when he became the principal acting teacher of our class.

From a very early age, I knew I wanted to be a part of the theater—not as an actor but, surprisingly and mysteriously, as a director. I was taken to many plays by my mother and various aunts and appeared in, wrote, and "directed" plays in grammar school and for my little troupe of players in one of my friend's backyards. My parents agreed to enroll me in acting class, which met on Saturdays near Rockefeller Center. A pretty, redheaded instructor handed us monologues, which we learned and performed while she sat with the script and marked with up and down arrows as to where the intonations should be.

When I heard about the High School of Performing Arts, I begged my parents to let me try for it, even though it meant traveling to midtown New York from our Brooklyn Heights apartment. The audition morning arrived; armed with two monologues, I entered a room in which a panel of faculty members sat, and with a pencil taking the place of a cigarette in an elegant holder, I channeled—or rather imitated—George Sanders in the opening monologue of *All About Eve*, to the effect that: "Margo Channing became a star at the age of eight appearing as a fairy in *A Midsummer's Night Dream*. She's been an actor ever since." (I myself was twelve.)

When the audition (which included an improvisation) was over, one of the judges said they couldn't tell me anything that day but added that I must not under *any* circumstances go back to that Saturday acting class ever again.

I was accepted at Performing Arts and the first two years were alternately exciting, bewildering, and upsetting. My mother died of cancer, my father remarried soon thereafter, I now felt a stranger at home, and the faculty at critiques made it clear to me that I would never be an actor. I lived in fear of the dreaded letter that was sent to students every six months informing them whether they could continue in the program or must transfer to another school.

I had always done the work, including improv, sense memory, writing down beats, and my "intentions" (even before I had done anything with my scene partner!), but apparently to no avail. Still, the chairman of the drama program saw something in me that made her believe there would be a place *somewhere* for me in the profession, and so I was allowed to remain.

Michael Howard began working with us in the third year. We began by *not* rehearsing the text, as I had been doing, but rather improvising extensively around it: We acted out the given circumstances rather than intellectualizing them (oh, how that word kept coming up for me!) and did various exercises in which we covered up the script, said our lines with an intention, and then listened to our partner without sure knowledge of what was to come next, allowing our response to exist before we read the next line. I think this was my first inkling of what "subtext" might mean and what "being in the moment" truly was. Michael insisted on a full relaxation exercise in advance of starting work on the scene and then a preparation of the circumstances *before the scene began*. Once, my partner and I, doing a scene in which we were supposed to be late for a ferry ride, left the school building (which was then on 46th Street), ran down to Broadway and back, entered the school (an accomplice was holding the door open), and arrived onstage, panting realistically, to make our boat ride. Luckily we were young and so still had enough breath to say our lines.

What was most crucial for me was to feel free to bring whatever was going on within—my internal state—into the scene. This work, which finally took me out of my head (which had been constricting me and making me direct and judge myself), began to gel under Michael's encouragement, and one miraculous afternoon, when my partner and I had finished a scene (of all things Pygmalion!), the feeling that it had all happened in the present—all spontaneous though rehearsed—filled my body and I knew what living on the stage could be. Subsequently, Michael surprised me by casting me in the Fourth Year Project, and upon graduation I received the Best Actor award—and the first wristwatch I ever owned.

I continued to study with Michael in his private evening classes when I was at Columbia University. One evening he took me aside and told me he was going to have to leave the class for a while in order to direct a play on Broadway and he wanted me to fill in for him. I was flattered but hesitant—many of the students were older than I was, but Michael's faith in me allowed me to say yes and so began a teaching career that has run side by side with my directing. Michael had taught me to act, which as a director has helped me to understand an actor's process, and now he was encouraging me to teach, and those skills have sustained my career throughout my artistic life.

Later, because I had worked for Michael in summer stock as an apprentice and as an assistant, it was one of the great joys in my life to offer Michael the lead in a production of two Ionesco plays that I would do off-Broadway in the spring of 1964, *Victims of Duty* and *The New Tenant*. Throughout the rehearsal process he was the actor and I was the director, and it seemed to have completed my process of becoming an adult.

I need to say one more personal thing. Michael was not only a mentor professionally; he, and his wife Betty, helped me through some difficult personal times. I "ran away" from home (it was only some five blocks from our apartment to the Howards' apartment in Brooklyn Heights) at the absurdly advanced age of eighteen. Michael and Betty allowed me into their home and then into their family. Even though I went back to my home after a few hours, I now knew that I had another family when I needed it.

I have many people to thank for an extraordinary life in the American theater: Edward Albee, who produced my first off-Broadway production; Joe Papp, who gave me my first Shakespeare play, inspired me with the possibilities of noncommercial theater, and ignited my desire to become an artistic director; and John Houseman, who invited me to join the founding faculty of Julliard as head of interpretation, which eventually led to my becoming director of the Drama Division for more than a decade. But it is Michael's patience, understanding, and commitment to truth that underlies most of what I have done and do.

I said at the beginning that this was a wise and generous book. Wise because it reveals the work that hundreds and hundreds of actors—many well known to us all from theater, films, and television—have experienced under Michael Howard's guidance. Generous because this work is now shared with all aspiring and working theater artists—not only technique and process but also the humanity and passion of this remarkable man.

A NOTE FROM THE AUTHOR

What impelled my writing this book is the astonishing experience of finding oneself, whether early in life or late, committed to accepting acting as a profession, to living the life of the actor. For many of us, that first mysterious jolt that led us into the profession can never be forgotten. This addiction—for this is what it seems to be—goes far beyond pseudo-psychological rewards. It may begin with the (universal) need for approval, but that cannot be what keeps one at acting, what keeps one addicted. After all, there is so little approval. There is mostly rejection. So there must be something else we get, we actors who stay the course.

There is no single answer, of course, to what keeps us in this career, despite a thousand excellent reasons to leave it. After seventy-odd years of a professional life in the world of acting and theater, I am still interested in the search, in the questions, and in some possibly shareable answers.

This is not a book about how to interpret a system of acting (usually Stanislavski's in the past ninety years), nor is it a "how to" manual that ends with a method (not even "The Method"). Many such books have been written, some excellent and useful, some foolish. Another one seems pointless.

Rather, this book is about how to make a life, how to live creatively and demand some pleasure from the chaos of the American theater, how to discover an enriched sense of self, and how to develop secret pride in the unexpectedly creative moment.

The personal anecdotes or stories of other actors I include here are aimed at stimulating an investigation into who we actors are and why we are—an investigation that I hope will resonate and remind.

I would like men and women who have done much more acting than I to read the book and say: "Yes, that's what I wanted from my life as an actor and that's what I still want." I want young, hopeful actors to feel encouraged to pursue this theatrical life and to give this book to their parents so that they will better understand why one would want to act.

There is no better community to live in than the theatrical community. No better place to recognize and accept the changes that take place in all of us as we mature. No better place to develop and maintain deep and enriching life-long relationships. Why this profession more than others? Read on . . .

Prologue

He made sure he was alone. He waited until nobody was near, nobody was watching, and then he stepped out of the doorway and walked quickly east on 89th Street. There was a pungent smell of horses coming from the stable across the street, and the sporadic clattering of hooves broke the silence that extended up to Central Park. Every few minutes, the elevated train roared above Columbus Avenue. Panting slightly by the time he turned the corner onto Columbus, he felt it necessary to stay in the shadows that fell like the black keys of a piano onto the sidewalk from the elevated tracks. The nine blocks to the Hotel Anderson on West 80th Street were uneventful. Inside, an elderly elevator operator dozed. Slipping by him was easy. In the back of the lobby, the switchboard lady, facing the plugs and jacks that connected her to each apartment and to the outside world, sat on her chair, reading a book. He walked up the two flights of stairs that surrounded the shaft of the open-cage elevator, looking down at the lobby to make sure he wasn't spotted. He moved quickly across the tiled third-floor hallway to an apartment with a "36" painted prominently on the door. The key, already in his hand, went into the lock. He turned the cylinder and pushed the door open, then stood in the doorframe for a long moment, listening and watching. He took the gun out of its holster and moved stealthily down the foyer hall. As he turned into the bedroom, the Other rose up from behind a chair and shot him. Mortally wounded and staggering, but with his own gun still dangling in his hand, he managed to get off one shot. One shot, but it was enough. He fell onto the bed, clutching his chest. He looked down, saw the blood spurting, and died . . .

. . . then I got up, went into the kitchen, and ate the milk and cookies my mother had left for me. Yes, that was me, a ten-year-old latchkey kid playing hooky, sneaking out of PS 166 on 89th Street, walking the nine blocks home to the Hotel Anderson, my head filled with fantasies of gangster movies, Pinocchio, and Oliver Twist.

Beginnings

How do you know you are an actor? Where does it begin, the desire to use yourself in this mysterious way? That fantasy was only one of many that helped me cope with a chaotic childhood. Is that kind of fantasy the beginning of an actor? Not for every child, certainly, but important it was to me and to my beginnings. For fantasy is what actors do—they pretend, they make believe, they imagine *Lies Like Truth*, as Harold Clurman titled one of his books. The actor must find a way to make the fantasies given to him by the playwright as connected, as important, and as necessary to himself as mine were to my ten-year-old self.

I grew up on the Upper West Side of Manhattan in the 1920s and '30s, during the Great Depression. My early childhood was a series of furnished single rooms, rented with a bed, bureau, chair, sheets, towel, and a bathroom down the hall shared with strangers. My father was not about, although every now and then he would appear, and he and my mother would fight. I remember their love-making, then their fighting, the violence, then the police; then we were forced to move. Of my father, I have these few memories: he wore knickers and two-toned shoes, and he drove a red Nash convertible. He worked in real estate, among many other things, and on rare visits took me to newsreel theaters and bought me clothes in S. Klein's On the Square, a now-vanished emporium on the east side of Manhattan's Union Square where those with little money shopped.

We moved a lot, up and down the West Side, until my mother and my aunt found an oasis for us: two rooms, a kitchenette, and the first refrigerator I ever saw. We had our own bathroom and a telephone (!) connected to that switchboard in the lobby of the Hotel Anderson. My mother, Gertrude, and my Aunt Sally were each barely five feet tall and supported themselves and me—when they could find work— as 100-words-per-minute typist-secretaries. I remember seeing my mother with a series of envelopes that contained parts of her weekly salary: one for "rent," another for "food," another for "carfare," and one labeled with my name, which always had five nickels.

My mother, feisty, funny, and graced with bright, questioning eyes, was the younger sibling by ten years. Inquisitive and supremely optimistic, she was sure there were great things ahead for her—and for me. My mother's great and enduring gift to me was that I never doubted I was a wanted child. Sally was the blonde, blue-eyed warrior, and her enemy was my father. When the three of us began to share the apartment on West 80th Street, he was forbidden entry. It was Sally who had paid Booth Salvation Army Hospital for my birth: $7.00—I have the receipt. Sally paid the biggest share of the rent and had the bedroom, while my mother and I slept in the living room. We dressed separately in the bathroom, which I also used as my reading room and the place where I could be alone.

Each sister had a small bookshelf. On Sally's, I remember an edition of *Salammbo*, a novel of ancient Carthage by Gustave Flaubert, which I read secretly, being especially drawn to the delightful illustrations of naked girls in orgiastic poses. My mother's shelf held eight volumes of Dickens, and I avidly read *David Copperfield* and *Oliver Twist* (twice). There was also a book by Arthur Schopenhauer ("Read it, it's interesting," she told me when I asked her about it; I was eleven). I also remember a book by a popular psychologist, Émile Coué, a Frenchman who preached self-help: "Want something badly enough? Say it out loud often and repeat it enough, and you'll get it!" It was a tome from which my mother loved to quote.

These two Jewish women were great assimilators. In the gentile business world of the 1920s and '30s, you either hid your Jewishness or risked dismissal, and my mother and Sally walked a fine line. My grandfather only spoke Yiddish at home, but his daughters were modern women. Christmas—and its presents—was the only holiday I remember celebrating. I had heard about Yom Kippur, but I knew next to nothing about it. Still, at my mother's insistence, I was bar mitzvah-ed (mostly in English) at the West End Synagogue on West 82nd street. In perhaps the greatest nod to assimilation, my mother and aunt were avid golfers (Sally had the clubs).

While my mother worked, I cut school. I hated school, and even now I can't tell you why; there seemed to be nothing there for me. I used fantasy—I needed fantasy—to deal with the fear of going into the Hotel Anderson, which was empty and quiet in the middle of the day because the grown-ups were at work (or more likely looking for work). Solo, I played out every scenario my imagination could cook up. I also remember climbing, circus-like, on the furniture in our room, from chair to bureau to bed, my feet not touching the floor, and when I was successful, taking a bow!

Too often, children are urged to put away such childish things ("Go play with your friends outside!"), and then the pleasure and the need to fantasize and to imagine can too easily be squashed. But some of us don't listen. The fantasies are too enriching, and using our imaginations is too pleasurable. This early joy in play-acting does not make an actor, but it can be the first, embryonic brick in the building of one. It was for me.

A few years after my "shoot-out" on 80th Street, I went to the Pioneer Youth Camp in Rifton, New York, near the Hudson River. It was the summer of 1935, and I was twelve. The camp changed my life. I see my existence before that camp in grays and black-and-white. Color began for me in that experience. I had my first feelings of love (she was twelve and looked like Judy Garland). There were many firsts for me, including singing with other people, dancing, and classical music. Huddie Ledbetter (Lead Belly) came and played for us!

I discovered friendship and felt less alone. When I enjoyed, I enjoyed with others; when I allowed myself to be foolish, all around me were other clowns; and when I was angry, there were others who understood and shared my ire. I discovered there was much to be angry about. Most of the other kids came from working-class, socialist-leaning families, and I think they took great pleasure in politicizing and acculturating me. I learned Socialist anthems like "I Dreamed I Saw Joe Hill Last Night." My Judy Garland look-alike introduced me to Mozart. This was a left-wing camp, operating on little money. Socialism was the flag we carried.

There was also a drama counselor, David Danzig, but this was definitely not the sort of place that put on Broadway musicals. I remember a little barn with a dirt floor. One day, Dave, who had big, heavy glasses and wore bellbottom dungarees, suggested an improvisation to a young girl and me. I had never done anything like that, of course. I didn't know what the word "improvisation" meant. But I remember the scenario he proposed: there was a young girl I cared about, my family was moving to another city, I would never see her again, and I had asked her to meet me in the park so I could tell her the bad news.

We began the improvisation. I was sitting on a bench, looking at her. I began talking to the girl as I never had talked to another human being before. I was suddenly uncovered, truthful. I was unafraid. I heard myself making up stories about how maybe, somehow, she and I could see each other again, visit each other, even if we were living hundreds of miles apart. Finally, we said goodbye. I think we hugged. She walked away. I sat there, stunned. I was full of conflicting emotions. I was angry, my heart was pounding, and I was breathing with difficulty. Where had all that come from? I had never experienced deep feelings like these, and I didn't understand them. Even as I write about it now, I can feel my memory sparking. Whatever had happened during that improvisation had touched some deep place within me that at age twelve I knew nothing about. Then I turned and looked at Dave Danzig. He was changed, he was different: eyes wide, mouth slightly open. What I saw in his face was a reflection of what I was feeling. He seemed surprised, and as moved as I was, though he said nothing. During that silence, I realized he had experienced what I had experienced; he was living it with me. More important, I felt that he had gotten me and was changed by me.

And there you have it, the keystone for me: becoming aware of the ability, the power, to affect others, to offer surprise, even insight. No longer was my fantasy life only between my ears; it could now exist in relation to another person. Affecting Dave Danzig was the beginning of my becoming an actor and embarking on a life in the theater. Because finally—more than money, more than dreams of glory, more than the desire for one's name on a marquee or spread across a movie screen—what draws an actor inexorably to acting and holds him there is the ability to affect another person, an audience, and, ultimately, the experience of being one with a thousand people.

After that summer, I secretly began to think of myself as an actor. In my second summer at Pioneer Youth Camp, we made a movie in Kingston, New York, about workers in the nineteenth-century brickyards. I played a strikebreaker, a villainous role. I remember hitting my friend Muriel Newman on the head with a club. Acting was now even more enriching when I could take pleasure in villainy—and in public! The years following that second summer offered experiences that continued to widen my sense of what being an actor meant.

In 1938, I saw a Broadway play called *The Greatest Show on Earth* from box seats someone had given to my mother. Wonder of wonders, all the characters in the play were animals, and of course they were played by actors. They created their characters not with furry coats and long ears and tails but with only their bodies. I was fascinated with how they moved, how they related to each other, how they rested, and how they fought. They did this solely through the craft of acting!

At the same time, some of my campmates (who were now my closest friends) decided to put on a play together in New York at a theater we would rent. We got the rights to *Three-Cornered Moon*, by Gertrude Tonkonogy, and we rented the Master's Institute Theater at 103rd and Riverside Drive. We did it all. Muriel directed, we all produced, and the show ran for three performances. It is difficult now to believe that such a lovely theater could have been rented by a group of kids, but that's exactly what we did. Many details of the production now escape me, for instance how much it cost. It couldn't have been very much, though, because none of us had money. I paid my share of the production expenses by selling ice cream in Central Park. I carried a large box with a strap across my shoulders; the ice-cream pops were kept cold by dry ice. I also worked at what was then a little delicatessen-grocery store on 81st and Broadway: the now-famous Zabar's.

What I remember most acutely about the performances is that there was a boy in the play a year or two older than I was—and he was a better actor. I found out that he was studying at the New Theater League School in New York, and I set my sights on studying there too. My time at Dewitt Clinton High School, and the hour-long subway ride each way, was becoming increasingly arduous. I began cutting classes, so many that I almost didn't graduate. I'd take the train to school. I'd walk up to the building doors. Then I'd turn around and go back to the elevated subway. Up the stairs I went and took the first train downtown, to Times Square and the movie theaters (and, I confess, the burlesque houses) on 42nd Street. I'd pay my twenty-five cents and watch movies until three in the afternoon, when I could go home. I was only thirteen, but I was never stopped, never accosted. I watched a movie called *Beau Geste* at least seven times. In the burlesque houses, I loved the naked girls, but at home, I would practice the famous routines of the "Top Bananas," the head-liner comedians. These experiences (and my mother's little library), more than anything else, were my real education.

At sixteen, I, too, was studying at the New Theater League School with John O'Shaughnessy, himself an actor and a good director. From him I first heard the name Stanislavski and read his *My Life in Art*. Most of the actors-in-training were older than I was, and the teachers were all working professionally in the theater. Toby Cole was there—she would become the famous editor and theater anthologist of, among other things, *Actors on Acting*; the playwright Ben Irwin was teaching there too, as was the director Lem Ward.

A year later Lem cast me in my first professional job—for money too! It was called *Zero Hour*, an anti-war, anti-fascist play in which I played a young man who wanted to go to Canada to join the Canadian Air Force and fight the Nazis. It was produced off-Broadway at 430 Lafayette Street, in the studio owned by Helen Tamaris, a famous American dancer-choreographer. (This pacifist play closed the day after Hitler invaded the Soviet Union, on June 22, 1941.)

During this period, my mother, recognizing the importance of the theater to me, felt as parents always do—that the young actor needs a "real" profession to fall back on. Thus graduating from high school was essential. Wanting to help me, she scraped together enough money to send me to a therapist. After many months of twice-weekly sessions, the therapist said to me, "You're right. You're an actor, and no one will ever ask to see your diploma. Don't get your diploma for them. Do it to prove to yourself you can do it. Then you must move out of your mother's apartment, get a job, and be with your friends."

My mother was devastated. She wrote the therapist a furious two-page, single-spaced letter, accusing that good man of the worst treachery. But I did graduate, and that summer I moved out. On the morning of the day I was leaving home, before she left for work, my mother, weeping, gave me a huge hug and at the door pressed something into my hand. I thought it was money. I thanked her, shut the door, and opened my hand. It was a condom.

I moved into a studio in Greenwich Village. My little room on Sullivan Street had a closet with a toilet and a small sink (I went to a friend's apartment to shower), a hot plate in a closet, and a fireplace. That fireplace was the most precious thing about my new home. It became the gathering place. No one else had one. We lit the fire and drank. We lit the fire and sang. We lit the fire and made love. On the corner was a newsstand that sold cigarettes at seventeen cents a pack. The vendor would open a pack and sell individual cigarettes for a penny apiece to people like us, smokers all, who couldn't afford a full pack.

There were five of us, actors and folk singers, struggling to define who we were individually and as a group and to learn what it meant to create a career. Two of them, Paul and Charis Bain, were married, and I now also observed, for the first time, the joy of a good marriage. Dolph Green, my closest friend since I was twelve, was a freshman at NYU in the theater program. He was young, handsome, and a leading man, and he reminded everyone of Orson Welles. Paul, a Canadian and senior to us by a few years, was a talented singer and part of the thriving folk song industry of the early forties. Charis was the most theatrical and perhaps the most talented of us all. She was a free spirit, demanding and challenging, and the woman who introduced us to the work of Eleonora Duse. Betty Sanders was a folk singer and one of the closest female friends I ever had. The two women attended the theater program at New York University with Dolph, which is how we all met. Though the other three were older than Dolph and I, they accepted us and helped us grow up. Shortly thereafter, Dolph and Charis left NYU to join the renowned Neighborhood Playhouse theater school.

In the summer of 1941, the five of us got jobs in the "Borscht Circuit," in New York's Catskill Mountains, at a resort called Pearl Lake Lodge, to work as the summer's entertainers. Each night we performed a different bill. We thought out the programs at the beginning of the week. Some were easy to put together—concert nights were always made up of songs in the repertoire of the three singers in our company. Variety nights included some of these songs and some improvisations we either made up or took from a book of sketches. The theater nights, memorized during the week, were one-act plays, sometimes short scenes from plays, sometimes improvisations. For variety nights, each of us was called upon to do something. I, for instance, put together two pantomimes: pretending to play a pinball machine and doing a Dr. Jekyll and Mr. Hyde transformation.

That summer changed our lives. We had forged strong relationships, we cared deeply about each other, and now we had taken it all into the heat of combat—artistic turmoil, night after day after night, struggling, succeeding, failing.

Back in the city that fall, Dolph and Charis harassed the Neighborhood Playhouse into offering me a scholarship, and I began studying with Sanford Meisner, the actor and teacher who had been one of the original members of the Group Theatre. The time I spent at the Playhouse studying with Sandy, Martha Graham, Louis Horst, David Pressman, Jane Dudley, and other talented teachers was difficult, and finally rewarding, and that experience has only become more useful as the years have gone on. It was difficult because I had never learned how to be a student or how to behave with a male power figure. Further, Meisner was testy; he resented (and rightly so) anyone thinking (as I did) that they could do his work while missing some of his beginning classes.

I was studying at the Playhouse when America went to war in 1941 after Pearl Harbor. I enlisted, and by attending the Army's Signal Corps School at night, I was able to continue my studies at the Playhouse by day. But there was no way for me to earn a living in my final year, to pay the rent and buy food. It was a serious dilemma.

Then one of my friends at the Playhouse, Mary James, came to my rescue. She had graduated from a Southern college before arriving at the Playhouse, and her parents had given her a station wagon as a gift. Mary decided she didn't need a car in New York and so she sold it—and gave me half the proceeds. Mary, the career-saver.

As soon as Dolph and I graduated from the Neighborhood Playhouse, we were inducted as full-time soldiers. Thinking we would make poor ordinary foot soldiers in a war we saw as necessary, and hoping to stay together, we volunteered for the Parachute Troops. Paratroopers wore jazzy uniforms—silk scarves, boots, and a great jump-jacket. It was quite theatrical. But I didn't see him again until the war ended; he was sent to the 17th Airborne, while I went to the 101st.

I went to Fort Benning, Georgia, for basic and then parachute training, which included weeks of exhausting and mind-bending physical training, as well as rigging our own parachutes, communications, and demolition. The last week consisted of five jumps, during the day and at night. Our joy, the excitement and the danger, and finally the accomplishment were not easily forgotten. Thrilled to get our wings, we held a big party with lots of beer. Someone tipped off the captain that I was an actor. He called me in and said, "Listen, Howard, we're celebrating tonight, we've got a drummer, we've got a singer, I want you to do something." I said, "Sir, I'm an actor. I'm not a comedian. I need a script." He said, "Now come on! Do it for your buddies. It's a party; it doesn't have to be great." Cornered, I remembered my pantomime acts in the Borscht Circuit. They had loved me in the Catskills.

The captain brought me on stage, in front of a few hundred fellow celebrants. The room was noisy. There had been much beer drinking. Yes, I thought, pantomime would be best. (Oh, foolish fellow!) I was nervous. I began with my pinball pantomime. Soon I realized the noise was getting louder, and louder still, and it became obvious I was dying up there. Somebody yelled, "Get him a Section Eight!"—the army code for the psychologically unfit. The audience thought that was funny and picked up the line, and the chanting of "Section Eight! Section Eight!" now echoed throughout the auditorium. It was getting a lot of laughs; they thought it was a lot funnier than what I was doing. I stopped. I yelled, "Okay, you're right. I'm going to pick up my Section Eight. See you guys later." I made for a hurried exit, but the captain, his authority threatened, grabbed me, pushed me back on stage, and then turned to the men and shouted, "You guys, shut up! Go ahead, Howard!" There was no way for me to escape. So I began my Jekyll-and-Hyde pantomime, pouring the potion, drinking it down. Now, they were really after me. I don't remember their words. My ears were blocked and I was pouring flop sweat. I went on for a little bit, and then I stopped, looked out at the crowd, and walked off. I walked right past the next performer, a guy with drums, past the captain, without a word, and then out of the building.

In vaudeville, what happened to me that evening was called "getting the bird." An audience turns on the performer and has more fun ridiculing than watching. The catcalling builds and there's no way to stop it. Comics know they can deal with one heckler, or even two, but not if the whole club, the whole theater, turns on the performer. I walked in moonlight down a Georgia country road for I don't know how long. Seventy years later, that "bird" is still fresh.

I tell this story because it speaks to what actors fear most. We do not consciously believe an audience will actually attack us, but our psyche won't listen. Making an entrance can be like going into combat and it, too, requires a kind of bravery. This is particularly true if you are a serious actor and the part demands that you reach down deep within yourself to reveal the character. Middling performers—those who close off, who keep themselves safe—are not so much at risk. But for the actor willing to reveal a most private self, the fear of getting the bird partly explains the complicated and contradictory emotions surrounding what is called "stage fright." To experience the excitement and anticipation of the entrance, the kick of the elevated heartbeat, and at the same moment the mindless fear of "the bird" is at the center of the actor's profession. Good performers develop an appetite for that always-exhilarating, sometimes-terrifying experience. Actors, over a period of years, find their own individual ways of dealing with this duality. It's astonishing, however, how often an unexpected attack of stage fright can rise up and bite the actor.

But never mind. In its own wonderful way, acting is an addiction. The continuing studies of self and craft, the development of empathy, the ability to sense what another human being is thinking, the capacity for intimacy—all are the gifts that the pursuit of an acting career can give to the man or woman who is willing to accept the challenge.

And nothing is more important than the capacity and pleasure of working within an ensemble, a company. It's best not to wait for one to find you: Find or help create a community of people who share your artistic goals, people who share your sensibility, whose talent and work you admire, and who respect, encourage, and admire you. Look for the company, the fellow actors—and the teachers—who recognize that acting is an art. An actor needs a community of sympathetic artists. Developing a deeply anchored acting talent is too hard to do all alone. It is possible to work creatively even in a world of strangers (there are times, of course, when we must), but if your fellow artists on a project remain strangers, if there is not some coming together over a common vision, the work loses something terribly important. The artists lose something too: the soul-satisfying pleasure—the physical kick—that comes from being in tune with each other. The world of the theater, including film and television, is at its root an ensemble undertaking.

I.

The Actor in the World

Chapter 1
The Actor in the World

For most actors—not all—there is a moment when a little light goes on, a spark occurs ("Maybe, this is who I am!"). Then it's a very long time later, if the spark isn't extinguished, that the actor realizes what he is asking: the willingness to reveal the brightest and the darkest parts of himself, to allow himself to be seen as foolish, fatuous, generous, heroic. It should scare him. If he is honest, it does. And he reveals by holding up the mirror, as has been famously said—not to reflect the casual moment, but rather so that they, the audience, can see themselves at the actor's most intimate, painful, and revealing moments. "This is you," the actor says, "This is you loving and lusting, hating and vengeful, winning and losing. This is you ridiculous and heroic." In a lightning flash come the heartiest laughs and the deepest internal weeping. "Yes," each audience member secretly thinks. "Yes, that is how it was." They recognize themselves and know without knowing that all the others who surround them in the audience have experienced their own secrets. This communal experience, the experience of being revealed to ourselves surrounded by others equally unzipped, can be life affirming, enriching, clarifying—and it is necessary. Necessary if we are to be human, truly and singularly human.

There are theater people who say, "It's the audience, pay attention to the audience, that's what matters." Of course the audience is important, but it is not about pleasing them or giving them their money's worth. It is about affecting them, changing them. What we, actor and playwright, do as theater artists is to say, "Listen, even if you came to the theater only to be entertained or to shed a sentimental tear, we want you to understand something. We want you to see yourself clearly. We want you, in spite of yourself, to be able to laugh at how foolish you are. To understand why it was so important for you to win, why you felt so rotten when you lost. We want you to recognize yourself in us. We want you to understand your life, with its hallelujahs and its hurts, as we hold the mirror up for you."

Do I place the bar too high? Why else would this art persist for millennia? I have even suggested for years to my students that Paleolithic cave drawings are set designs done by a shaman, priest, hunter . . . and actor. Standing in front of these paintings, he told of the glories, the fears, the near death, and the kill in the hunt. Perhaps his acting out in the firelight against those images on the walls helped cave dwellers understand what they had just experienced. Yes, I believe we are needed. The Athenians knew they needed us: Behind the mask we went, our voices magnified, searching into their very souls. Even before Shakespeare shook the world, we went out from the churches and into the streets with liturgical dramas and mystery plays, helping to overcome the dark and to laugh at the devils. And, yes, eons ago, when one of us in that cave stood up before the fire, his shadow cast large on the stone behind, and acted out the hunt, the watchers better understood their courage. We were needed then; we are needed now.

PERFORMERS AND ACTORS

The actor is part of a large family of performers, those who stand up in front of an audience wanting to affect them, to light them up, to excite them. It is a family with many branches. There are the glorious musicians and the dancers, who probably were the original performers. The drummers came first, almost forcing the dancer to invent dance, then the strummers, then the blowers into a reed. The singers added sound and melody. One branch of this family is circus performers, who enchant us to this day. There is the clown, and then there are acrobats and jugglers, who thrill us with daring and physical skill. It is a world without language. They make us experience dread and danger, as well as make us laugh. We worry for them, fear that they'll fall, and giggle when they slip on the banana peel. But . . . it is not about us. A sword swallower or a fire-eater who seems to be placing himself in jeopardy makes us fear for him and wonder at him, but it is not about us. We don't for a moment see ourselves swallowing swords. The man who does tricks with poisonous snakes wants us to worry and to recognize his daring. He affects us by his risk-taking, but it is not about us.

Then there is the actor, part of that family of performers, but very much his own category, his own species. The actor wants us, the watchers, to see ourselves mirror-like in all our wonder, our heroism, our foolishness—yes, it is about us.

The actor's tools—his physical and emotional tools—are there to accomplish this miracle of transformation night after night, play after play. The actor needs, and the profession demands, the strong performing instinct that comes with the development of both inner techniques and physical skills. The fully developed actor wants to juggle,

5

walk the tightrope, clown, and dance, and of course a large part of what makes an actor is that she must develop a wide-ranging vocal instrument: the grunts, the growls, the highs and lows, the almost-song, then, finally, the expressive use of language—all that and more. At her best, the actor wants to create, inspired by a challenging text and her own internal response, so detailed, so truthful, and so specific another human being that no matter the culture of the audience, he will experience, with pain or with pleasure, elements of his own life.

THE ACTOR-ARTIST

There are many kinds of actors and many kinds of acting. Remove your own concepts of what is good acting or what is bad acting, or for that matter what is great acting or what is vulgar exhibitionism. Even put aside an actor's particular way of working. For the moment, I am not discussing "how" the actor works but "what" the actor wants for himself out of his creative work-life, what he wants to give when the curtain goes up.

What is the difference, then, between what the young men and women, like Snooki and the Kardashians, who create what are ludicrously called "reality shows," do and what Laurence Olivier did? Is there any difference? Are they all involved in the same craft, the same career? The Screen Actor's Guild calls them all actors. The Internal Revenue Service calls them actors. Sir Laurence and the Kardashians think of themselves as actors. Even the audience thinks of them as actors, thinks that what they do is acting.

I suggest they have totally different careers, different aims, different tools, want totally different end products—even, stretching the concept, in the same way a plumber differs from an electrician. The craft is totally different. The tools the plumber uses have nothing in common with the electrician's wire cutters. They are both building a house, but there the similarity ends. Perhaps you will say I'm giving reality TV celebrities too much credit. After all, the plumber and the electrician are highly skilled, each in his own way. And I would agree. The whole concept of a so-called "reality show" denies reality and creates caricatures. Presumably, those celebrities do what is asked of them very well (or hundreds of thousands of people wouldn't watch it every week). But I suggest what they do is a different profession entirely.

Olivier searches—as all good actors do—for transformation. From Richard III to Shylock to Archie Rice in *The Entertainer*, he wants the experience of revealing hidden elements that exist in himself and in the great villains and heroes of the world. And, of course, as a star he was given the opportunity to accomplish total transformations. Genius and non-genius actors alike make the same demands of themselves. They are concerned with transformation, not with celebrity.

Still, there are enormously talented, highly gifted, craft-competent actors who allow themselves to be used exactly the way Snooki is using herself. The industry finds one desirable, unusual trait that the very good actor is asked to repeat, over and over again. There is nothing new or unacceptable about this. Audiences sometimes demand it of great stars (historically, on stage and in film) and they, in turn, have potboilers written especially for them. (Eugene O'Neill's father, a fine man of the theater, was destroyed by acceding to the audience's demand for *The Count of Monte Cristo*. He continued to play the same part for very many years until he realized how little of the artist was left in him.) For actors can only flourish and realize themselves fully when allowed to play different kinds of people in different cultures, with different body languages, different speech patterns, in both poetry and prose. Of course, actors will not refuse another cop-part, another pratfall-silly sitcom. At all levels of acting, making a living often takes priority. A long time ago, that same Sir Laurence Olivier shocked all of us "serious actors" by being the first "serious actor" to do a commercial. When asked "why?" it is reported that he answered with asperity, "I have children on the way to college." But even while earning a living, actors must continue to deepen, to explore, to find nuance and surprise even in the most superficial material.

What unearths truth is what the actor—rejecting the easy and the conventional—demands of himself. That demand, that insistent, unrelenting search in the text and in himself, is what creates the Actor-Artist. It is a demand that is strong at the beginning of an artist's career and logically gets stronger and more robust with maturity; it must never be allowed to slip away. ("It takes twenty years to become an actor," said Sanford Meisner—an actor-artist, that is.) The actor-artist begins to create art—rather than convention—when he realizes the great pleasure, satisfaction, even joy in recognizing that there is something hidden, secret, and more revelatory waiting for him to uncover. This realization and therefore the commitment to take what the writer has given and by some extraordinary internal alchemy to reveal some aspect of the human condition—in a thousand different ways for a thousand different actors—is what creates art.

Though actors have always complained about the profession (and often for good reason), the truth is actors love acting. The excitement of a suddenly revealed answer is the same for the man playing a foot soldier sitting at the fire as it is for the actor playing Henry in Shakespeare's *Henry V* (or as we actors/soldiers in World War II, having spent much time in France, called it, "Hank Cinque"). Olivier was asked by the British government to make a film of *Henry V* as a propaganda piece in order to rouse the English public's patriotism in the face of a potential invasion by Hitler. And he did it. A brilliant film, edited by him, produced by him, directed by him, with him playing the lead. A very big deal. A huge responsibility. And you know what else he did? In that film, he also played three Frenchmen—huge costume changes, makeup changes, much time. Yes. He plays the lackey who leads—dances, really—the French barons to their horses. He also plays another Frenchman who, before the night of Agincourt, comes into the French baron's tent whispering, "My lord high constable, the English lie within fifteen hundred paces of your tents" (Act III, Scene 7). That was Olivier! And yet again, on the day the conquering Henry is to appear in the French court, an attendant moves forward and holds a mirror for the French king. The king slaps his hand impatiently. That attendant was Olivier!

There are other characters that Olivier assumed in the film, all Frenchmen. Why did he do it? With all the other responsibilities, why take the time? Because acting, particularly when we come to it without weighty responsibilities, gives pleasure, gives rest, gives surcease. Because acting, when they let us do it, is just fun, and it's a way of life.

You may ask how I know the background of that spectacular production. The distribution of Olivier's *Henry V* in the United States was accomplished by the Theatre Guild. And the Theatre Guild, well versed in road companies and in what were called "four wall deals," rented theaters across the country. People like me—actors—were hired to go from town to town, with the film in the can under my arm, with advertising material for the newspapers and posters and window cards to help bring an audience into the theater. I placed the ads, set up the box office, organized appearances, and spoke (not to say lectured) at high schools and colleges to discuss the film for the four days that it would be showing in a theater, twice a day. By my best count, I saw the film twenty-three times!

Only the very best of us can do it all: the brilliant conception and the totally realized execution—and that includes being internally connected to the deepest psychological character-truth and creating logical physical behavior that is specific and illuminating. Not only do it, but do it brilliantly. Even the great ones are unable to do it night after night, take after take. It isn't easy. Excitingly, those Mozarts that we aim to emulate often put the hurtful and the hilarious in the same character. Chaplin did it. Recently, Mark Rylance, playing a marvelously stylish, jokey, physically foolish Olivia in Shakespeare's *Twelfth Night* made me laugh just as I was moved, concerned about her romantic predicament. I cared about her. In the 1920s, John Barrymore was a New York–shattering Hamlet and a hilarious farceur in the play *The 20th Century*. In 1945, Olivier in one night brought Oedipus to Broadway and, after intermission, played the title role of Mr. Puff in Richard Sheridan's *The Critic*. My goodness. Both were stunning. As a young actor, how I ached to be able to do it.

THE LIE OF THE THEATER

Our profession, The Theater, begins with a lie. It is a lie that asks the audience to believe the actors are who they pretend to be.

And yet, during a performance, when a good actor-artist uncovers some unexpectedly illuminated human experience (imagined by the writer and given life by the actor), the whole audience, all one thousand of them, stops the casual coughing and holds its breath—struck to the heart by a revealed "truth." The audience has gone along with the superficial, laughed, even wept a sentimental tear, then suddenly there is the deepest connection between the actor and the audience. And the audience knows it. (Bless them, they know it.)

What is it that the actor-artist has done to scorch them, that gets behind their public mask? What kind of truth is the actor-artist searching for exactly as he investigates and constructs a role?

THE SPECIFIC VERSUS THE GENERAL

A human moment that is idiosyncratic, particular, surprising—specific—is understandable beyond language and beyond culture and is, in fact, universal. The nonspecific, the general, bleeds into the most superficial and conventional acting. That's the lie. The particular, the specific, is truth.

Truth for the actor is elusive, but it is not an abstract idea. Truth demands the particular response within the circumstances of the play. The actor is searching for the particular truth of that particular character in that particular moment.

REAL VERSUS NATURAL

In his pursuit of theatrical truth, should the actor concern himself with being honest, sincere, and natural? I say "No." As the actor works, he no longer has to question whether he's honest or sincere, because he has developed both an awareness of when he's lying and the ability to stop it. He has learned to recognize when he is only indicating emotional truth and to reject it. The media asks for—and actors try to be—"natural." A serious error. What is wanted is reality.

What is the difference between natural and real? Natural is general. Reality demands the specific. In his private class a long time ago (before the Studio), Lee Strasberg gave an example of the difference between what is real and what is natural, which I am adapting here:

11

If you shot a film of, say, Michael Howard, for twenty-four hours—filming every single thing he did from the moment he woke up to the moment he went to sleep, and all through the night—there would not be a moment that would be made up. (Best if Michael didn't know he was being filmed, I suppose.) It would be naturalism, *The Natural View of Michael Howard.* Then, if someone took that film and chose from it fifteen minutes—chose them with insight, discretion, and taste—the exact, perfect fifteen minutes that defined Michael Howard—which would be more truthful: the twenty-four-hour film or the fifteen minutes? Which would be more real? I think there's no question the fifteen-minute film would be more real, more important, more to the point, more exactly who Michael Howard is. Of course, another artist choosing fifteen minutes might make very different choices, creating a very different reality, a different truth. That is what an actor-artist does; it is what a director, an editor, a painter does—each one choosing specific details, selecting those elements that add up to reality (not naturalism) and truth: art.

TRUTH

Wait a minute. What is this "truth thing" I'm talking about? How do you discover within yourself and within the character that "truth"? How do you search for it?

I want to share with you the particular experience that helped me understand the discovery and revelation of personal truth. Just for me. I think every worker in the arts understands it but lives it differently.

In Florence, on the way to see the extraordinary sculpture of David, Michelangelo's blessed celebration of mankind, there are in the hall of the Accademia where the David stands four of his other sculptures.

Presumed to be unfinished, they show four slaves struggling to emerge from the stone in which they are entrapped. Michelangelo said they were always in the stone; he simply removed enough marble for them to emerge. The truth of these muscular, struggling figures to live, to be present, to be revealed to us, was always there. Michelangelo's use of his hammer and chisel seems to me to be an apt metaphor for the actor's process, which is at its essence to reveal. Of course, when the search into the stone is resumed and the truth is fully revealed, at the end of the artist's work there is the David.

It's a lovely idea for the actor: that the character, or the moment, is already within you, waiting for you to reveal it. Sometimes you are not a good sculptor and don't know what to carve away to make the work emerge. Sometimes the work emerges without too much effort; you chip away and there it is. Sometimes the revealing is difficult; at other times, it is easy. But always you sense that the specific thing to be revealed is already present within you and wants only to be given life. The truth that the actor-artist searches for—character-truth, relationship-truth, situation-truth—is there, in the text and in the actor. The actor's job is to set it free.

AIM

The actor wants, in maturing, to become familiar with, and be able to access, all the positives and negatives of his elastic temperament: sensibility, empathy, outrage, a sense of humor, unreasonable fear, courage, even wisdom. All of these are a necessary part of theatrical talent. The difficult thing is knowing how to access them and, in the theater, how to access them on demand and to bend them into the shape of the play. To transform them into art.

Talent is nothing without craft. Art wants craft, and craft must

13

have work—hard work—years and years of it. Craft demands strength without strain, developed powers of concentration, stamina, actors' will, self-awareness. And experience. It takes time, actor-work does, and the willingness to reveal secrets. And practice. Actors must act. Finally, and perhaps most urgent, actors must aim.

Aim is what enticed you into a life in the theater. Aim closed the door (or left it only slightly ajar) to other things. Aim is the road, unmarked and challenging, that carries the dream of a life in the theater. It stretches out in front of the hopeful with only the most misty, hallucinatory, ever-changing sense of where it will lead. This aim, this dream that the actor holds close, fantasizes about, is the heartbeat of a career. The actor must never lose sight of it. There are detours, wrong turns, necessary side trips that sometimes seem endless, barricades that must be breached. Aim encourages keeping on. It means doing work in a no-money, mediocre play but with a very good director who challenges you. It means accepting a wonderful play with a not-very-promising ensemble, with a nagging director, but with a risk-filled character that will stretch you. Perhaps most important, you will seek out like-minded colleagues who satisfy your hunger and encourage your appetite. And help you keep on.

Then there is the aim, the artistic hope, as you work on a part. You have a view of what excites you, of how specific the character can be. Keeping yourself uncloseted, searching for things not clearly defined, welcoming sudden opposing views—these can create exceptional surprises. Aim is a door opener to the unexpected answer. Within the struggle for that answer, there is disappointment, hopelessness, and also the "hallelujah" moments—celebration, exultation, and, even if only for a moment, quiet self-love. (As Shakespeare says in *Henry V*, Act IV, Scene 2, "Self-love, my liege, is not so vile a sin as self-neglecting.")

THE REAL WORLD

Let me be practical. Put theory aside. Put philosophy aside. Put aesthetic desires aside. Aim has to include real-world considerations: to make a living, have a family, live decently. What the actor really wants every waking hour is work. Any kind of acting work, in anything, anywhere, in any medium. It is printed on the flag the actor carries. Work for bread, yes. And work for growth and development.

The aim, the dream for a career actor, should be to have it all, the best, and I'm not talking about success and applause—the Tonys and Oscars. I'm talking about the most exciting challenges that the theater provides. The very young actor, as she negotiates the first urgings of wanting to "perform," sees herself as able to transform, to become, if you will, different people, in different worlds—old and young, dangerous and saintly, lustful and "Mary"-like. This young actor, as she goes to grad school (or doesn't, but rushes off to Hollywood or New York), still remembers, still holds to that first, strong, inner thrust.

Then the real world intrudes. She still wants it all—Aeschylus, Shakespeare, Ibsen, Molière, Coward, Tennessee Williams—still wants transformation, whether in theater, film, or TV, but what takes over is creating a career and making a living wage. "Osric in Hamlet, in a garage?" (Yes, why can't a woman play Osric?) "No thanks, I have five lines on *Law and Order* and it pays the rent for a week." Of course, you must. But it is not why you were called to this profession. Next time, do Osric. Do an extraordinary, flashy, physically truthful Osric. And get the laugh. It's why you are here. Don't you remember?

15

A young, talented, and handsome man will now stand up and say, "Excuse me, sir, but from the beginning I wanted only to be famous, to have a long-running commercial or an ongoing part on a night-time series playing that cop and make a lot of money." I will say, "Good luck, I wish you only the best. How very lucky that you have found what you wanted. I hope they find you." I mean it. It is worthy and honest. Worthwhile.

But if you were driven into this unyielding profession by some other want, some other imagined life, then you must fight for it, you must dig in your heels. The struggle to find it—that struggle itself—is what is finally fulfilling. There is no roadmap, except for the one you yourself will make.

Chapter 2
Techniques, Styles, and Methods in a Changing Society

In the world of the theater, what was acceptable and critically applauded in 1914 on Broadway and in the popular theaters across the country and the Western world is today justifiably laughed at and ridiculed. The stories were superficial melodramas, with Villains! Heroes! and Saintly Children! and always happy endings. Understandably, audiences wanted to look at pretty pictures, the idealized life of Virtue Rewarded, Villainy Punished, and not the truth of the real world that surrounded them with twelve-hour workdays and child labor. They wanted the storybook picture. They wanted to have the experience of crying sentimentally, not the shock of truth waiting outside. Here in New York, the theater was consciously oblivious to the real world that existed one block west of Broadway in Hell's Kitchen.

The acting was equally superficial. Presentational and illustrative worldwide, it was defined by a Method—the Delsarte Method—which prescribed exact physical gestures for each emotion. There were practiced gestures that everyone used to express the broken heart and righteous rage. There were also good actors who found inventive and idiosyncratic new ways of expressing behavior. These moments were called "Points." Actors might find creative ways to fall to their knees or draw their sword, and these "Points" were written about and critically applauded. Whatever the value of Delsarte's investigation into the physicalizing of internal emotional experience, his Method created onstage puppets, not people. Delsarte's useful questions were compromised by the fact that his Method was eagerly accepted worldwide, taught badly, and inevitably caricatured—not an unusual fate for "Methods."

All theater is a product of the society in which it lives. When society is in flux, the theater is in flux. When society wants to hide, the theater hides. Except for the exceptions. And exceptions there were, demanding that we look at and experience (even laugh at) the real world and change it. These exceptions showed us a way to know better who we are and who we want to be: Shaw, Ibsen, Chekhov, Strindberg. And actors, too: Duse, Chaliapin, Salvini, Le Gallienne, Barrymore, and Booth.

In the acting profession, the argument that has promoted change, upset apple carts, instigated fisticuffs, and for hundreds of years brought forth numberless scholarly works has as its concern—unbelievably—the actor's process: Shall the actor work to present, to illustrate with art and imagination, a perfect picture of a person involved in an emotional trauma? Or shall the actor attempt to experience the situation and relationship that will bring, with equal art, the required and deeply realized result? Experiencing, it should be said, does not mean reenacting literally what is written but rather understanding, recreating, and internalizing the larger truth that drives the character. This argument goes back hundreds of years, even before James Quin, a rigorously classic major star of the eighteenth century, who, when he saw David Garrick, a newcomer, attempt simple naturalism, famously said: "If this young fellow be right, then we have all been wrong." Quin was correct: He was wrong. Toward the end of the century, the arguments continued with John Phillip Kemble, a magnificent "presenter," on one side and his sister, Sarah Siddons, an "experiencer" (and the most revered artist of her time), on the other. She was followed by Edmund Kean in the first part of the nineteenth century who went even further in "living through," actually frightening audiences by bringing such truthful emotional fierceness that people fainted.

At the end of the nineteenth century, Konstantin Stanislavski, responding to the Delsarte Method and to the illustrative work he saw even in the most talented actors in the Russian theater, began to question, to explore, how the exceptions—the great actors who seemed to be living through, to be experiencing rather than presenting—accomplished their work. To better understand their processes so as to devise a system for all actors to use, he studied, at length, the great actors of his time: Duse, Salvini, and many others who came to Moscow.[1] At the center of Stanislavski's evolving system, which he continued to develop for the rest of his life, were ways of researching physical actions and translating affective memories into accomplishable tasks, as well as the need to be totally present, to experience, emotionally and physically, the heightened imaginary world given to the actor by the playwright, and never to indicate or illustrate emotional truth.

As I have said, acting styles change, influenced by the society in which we live. The ways the theater asks the actor to behave are themselves constantly changing. It took twenty years for Stanislavski's

---

1. Stanislavski, Constantin, *My Life In Art* (Boston: Little, Brown and Company, 1924), p. 463.

system to reach America and to begin to work its cataclysmic change, and it is still evolving. Only after World War I, the Russian Revolution, and finally the visit of the Moscow Art Theatre in 1922 did the evolutionary change begin to take root in the American theater. It began with Richard Boleslavsky, who created the American Laboratory Theatre in New York in 1923. But Stanislavski's processes, extended by Boleslavsky, were not widely taught and did not yet affect the American theater community.

In 1929 came the Depression, and all the ideas of who we Americans were and what we thought we had accomplished blew up in our faces. Their replacement was a new and harsh reality: strikes and strikebreakers, no jobs, no food, and no money. Theater artists—writers in particular—responded to this new world—tough, dirty, magnificent, painful. Actors now had to learn to work differently, to connect themselves to, and reveal, the unpleasant truths they were living every day. Some members of the Laboratory Theatre, Lee Strasberg and Harold Clurman among them, founded the Group Theatre, which demanded of itself not only that it mirror this new world, but also that it investigate and practice Stanislavski's system to help reflect, and even affect, this world. Clifford Odets, an actor in the Group Theatre, began writing plays about the world as it was. Harold Clurman and Lee Strasberg, as well as Stella Adler, Sanford Meisner, Bobby Lewis, and Morris Carnovsky, brought their already established careers to this new way of working. As actors, teachers, and directors, they became major influences on future generations of theater artists.

AND THEN CAME TECHNOLOGY

. . . And new worlds for the actor to discover.

In 1923, the same year that Boleslavsky was creating the

American Laboratory Theatre, radio was born. That same year the movie found its voice, and "talkies," the first talking motion pictures, were invented. Its cousin, television, had to wait, but only until 1927 before its official unveiling, and it was another twenty years before it was commercially available. The decade of the twenties, more than any other ten-year period, saw the most significant changes in the long history of the profession of acting: in the use of the voice, the use of the body, and even the use of the internal instrument.

Before the talkies, the still emerging motion pictures wanted everything the actor could bring—except the voice: Think of the wonderful physicality of Charlie Chaplin and Buster Keaton. Then came radio, and it wanted only the voice; the beautiful looks and physical adroitness that actors had spent years developing were no longer required. Suddenly, actors were having careers relying only on their voice. My first acting job in the larger commercial world was in radio. It was 1940, and, needing guidance, I ran to Norman Rose, a wonderful stage actor who now had a major career in radio: "How? How do I do this?" He answered, very simply, "Just do it like you'd do it if you were telling a child a good story, then make it as truthful to yourself as you can." I also saw, when I watched a pro like Norman work, that just because the medium "only" needed the voice, it didn't mean that the rest of his body wasn't involved. In radio, no memorization was required. With his script in hand, the microphone in front, and the sound-effects man right next to him, Norman's body was always helping, wanting to be involved.

There were big changes when the talkies arrived. Great motion picture stars from the previous decade had to pack up and find other careers, because their voices were so unrelated to their looks. Leading men with high-pitched voices and exotic women with the accent of the streets were no longer acceptable. But talking pictures—what became known as "film"—were here to stay.

Perhaps the most monumental challenge in the world of performing came with the development of the film industry. New careers began. Film directing became a new profession and the industry belonged to the director. Men and women who had never been involved in the theater often took hold of this new medium and developed it. And once again, the actor had to adapt.

AND TELEVISION?

Television and I grew up together. When I joined Actor's Equity in 1947, the medium was barely out of the lab. In the late 1940's, DuMont Television, a New York–based local television station, as well as CBS and NBC, were beginning to produce live shows in this new "thing" using actors. For many of us it meant paid work here in New York. It was live, it was exciting, and it was primitive. It was like off-, way off-, off-Broadway is now. There were of course very few TV sets—even in the fifties people would gather in front of store windows to watch major events. No one I knew owned a television set, so neither I, nor friends or family, could see me work. Perhaps it was just as well.

DuMont had a series called *Buck Rogers in the 25th Century*, and I was somebody's favorite Martian. Favorite because I was hired three times to do it. Or maybe I fit the costume. It was "live" television, with all the attendant mishaps. Soon, much like a run-down neighborhood, creative people moved in and changed what was for them a wide-open landscape. Good writers ran to it: Paddy Chayefsky, Rod Serling, Norman Corwin—and good actors followed. Far better and more experienced actors than I were drawn to it. Experimenting, testing, failing, succeeding—the fifties were an exciting time. Those television years were a school, a learning place for everyone: sound, lighting, camera people, as well as writers and directors. Sidney Lumet, then a well-known young actor, resigned his day job teaching at the High School for the Performing Arts in 1951 (I took his place) to work as an assistant director for a television network. Curious theater professionals needed to discover what this new medium was all about.

Actors, especially, had to take everything they knew and now include or, harder still, ignore the camera. Those of us who were raised in the theater on improvisation were fortunate. There was no stopping, no do-overs. It was exciting. Like live theater? Not really. The sets were tiny, the cameras not very mobile, and everyone and everything was in a hurry. There was no scene changing. I remember getting shot, and as I lay inert, the crew cut to a thirty-second scene of someone telling my mother, then back to me in the hospital bed. I almost got caught, fully dressed, hopping into that bed.

And then the product sellers, the corporations, drawn by the excitement, concerned about attracting the largest numbers to buy their soap, took over. Logically, they were disinclined to shock, disturb, or encourage anything considered boat-rocking. Serious writing, challenging ideas, and chance-taking were discouraged. The medium now belonged to the product-makers and their advertisers. But creative people kept trying. The medium itself, with all its new technical challenges, was irresistible. And there was work, paid work, for actors and writers.

In the 1950s came the blacklist. That list and all that came with it not only destroyed lives and careers, it ended, for years, television as a creative arena for tough-minded, out-of-the-box writers and all of us who depended on them. Writers who were not blacklisted began to self-censor. Don't make waves. Keep your head down. Careful, careful. It was, as it was called, a wasteland. Not until American newsmen like Edward R. Murrow, who were willing to speak truth with courageous objectivity, did television and the nation begin to right themselves.

Always, there were extraordinary exceptions. Wonderful actors managed (as they always have) to make silk purses when all that was asked of them was to help sell toothpaste. Comedians, particularly, with the help of comedy writers, took the medium of television and made it their own. They gave television a profile, a reason for being. Television gave us the joy of Jackie Gleason and Lucille Ball. A few comedians, like the Smothers Brothers and Rowan and Martin, tried to make waves and push content to the edge, but they were quieted. But overall television did for comedic actors what moving pictures did for Charlie Chaplin and Buster Keaton. It did what vaudeville tried to do in the nineteenth century and radio in the early part of the twentieth—it brought these great talents right into our homes week after week, accessible and live.

The arrival of cable brought a sea change in television. Rough water is now allowed. Chance-taking. Storms. Danger. Once again good writers, given free rein, are at the helm. For the first time, television is asserting its right to be considered a serious venue for the best creative people. Not only writers and producers but also the best actors, in good and challenging stories, and surrounded by other good actors, and given unhurried time, are finding creative pleasure, week after week, in developing deeply wrought characters and relationships. Once it was only in the theater, the live theater, where actors could find a community in which to live and grow, in which old ideas and the status quo could be challenged. Now, cable and all the new technologies assert themselves. It's an exciting time for actors. There is both aesthetic satisfaction and career exposure, and cable is willing to pay for it.

However, in considering all these new and exciting possibilities that television (and film, as well) offer, it is essential to understand that these technologies do not belong to the actor. Actors are an essential part, but these media are not theirs. Film belongs to the director and to the editor. Even the writer is not usually part of the hierarchy. Obviously, there have always been good writers and directors in film who created work of great meaning and interest, and in which an actor could feel he was contributing significantly to the work, but the medium does not belong to him. In television, writers begin to gain more importance, but still, technologists and directors own it. The actor must share the spotlight, must allow others—directors, editors, directors of photography, and more—to choose which piece of them, which moment of the many the actor has generously given them, will be the one that they—and not the actor—prefer. That one piece of the actor, chosen by all the others, is then frozen in time.

Only the live theater belongs to the actor. Only in the live theater, at 8:00 p.m., as the houselights dim, does everyone present—the director, the producer, the writer—know that it is up to us, the actors. So do we. This medium, this night, is ours. No cable TV show, no film, no animated technology has the one thing that changes all the rules, silences all the talk, alters the heartbeat: the audience. In front of a live audience, the actor makes all the choices, good or bad, for that one night. For those ninety minutes, or often much longer, there is nothing between the actor and the audience. The audience experiences the actor, sharing his joy, his pain, and even his foolishness, not at any moment in time, but now, alive. It is the live theater that gives the actor the potential for changing, and for evolving, truth every night.

But no matter the medium, no matter the technical demands—telling stories with no voice or only voice, no body or only the body—no matter the historical period, no matter the changing demands of audiences, the actor must bring his basic instrument to work: imagination, sensibility, his nervous system, a sense of logic, a sense of truth. New things are coming that are not yet imagined, new technologies and new social movements will change acting, and actors will again have to adapt. And they will.

Chapter 3
The Loneliness of the Long-Distance Actor and the Need for Community

Many different kinds of people look seriously to the theater and to acting as a life's work. There are those who train diligently, work hard at the business of acting, and get some work, even a great part, which should change everything . . . but doesn't. Then, at some point, perhaps after the second or third year of disappointments and small successes, and maybe even after the fifth year of trying to move forward in New York and remain an actor, a moment comes when, tired of waiting tables, he says, "The hell with this. I want a life. I can't do this. They don't let me do it. They don't want me." That actor says, "There are other things I can do. And I'm going to do them. I thought I could make an acting career, but I don't care enough. I want a life." And that actor leaves. Too often it is a very good actor, one the theater ought to encourage and give work to.

There is, however, another actor, who looks at the same unrewarding landscape and says, "I don't care. I'm going to do this. This is who I am. Good, bad, get work, don't get work, wait tables, bartend, I don't care. It's what I do, it's what enriches me. I refuse to give it up, and with or without recognition or 'success,' I am going to make a life in the theater."

That's who the long-distance actor is, and with it comes loneliness. The unemployed actor is the loneliest person in the world, it seems to me, because he needs other people so desperately to be able to do his work. I believe that is true for most performing artists. For most other professions, what matters when you are jobless, primarily and sometimes solely, is the paycheck. Of course, the actor wants to be paid (and paid well), but what comes first is the work itself, and that can mean little or no money at all. But it's work, and when an actor gets work, that special actor-loneliness, for the moment, is over. The long-distance actor wants and needs what he's already tasted, and that is the community: the getting together in the room in the morning and working openly and creatively, the ensemble. That's something that perhaps is true in other professions, but it strongly defines the life of the actor, and, once experienced, it is one of the elements that holds the actor in the profession.

THE FAMILY

In 1967, my wife, Betty, and I were preparing Thanksgiving dinner for our family. We decided to invite one of our oldest friends, a fine actor, Ruth Manning. Recently divorced, she had no family in New York. She was working on Broadway in a play called *You Know I Can't Hear You When the Water's Running*. There was no Thanksgiving matinee; we could have dinner and I could get her back to the theater before the evening performance. Perfect. She'd love it.

When I called her, she said, "Oh, thank you, Michael, but I'm having Thanksgiving with my family." Family? I didn't know she had any in New York. "No, darling, I mean the show, the company family." The company family. She was choosing her fellow actors over close friends who had known her for thirty years. Ruthie's response stopped me cold. The idea of family, of the company as family, of the intimacy that such an idea suggests, made me aware of an experience I myself had had before but never examined.

The possibility of this kind of "family" connection begins the first day of rehearsal, from the moment actors are brought together at someone else's command and then asked to create a work of art within a limited time. Even in a small part, an actor for the next few months finds that all else in his life becomes secondary. The actors, as they begin working together, develop a whole new set of relationships. At home, husbands and wives try to understand, but it's not easy. The actor's nose is in the script. The center of his life has become the rehearsal hall. It is difficult for actors not to bring the make-believe world home with them—especially the new aspects of themselves that emerge as they draw closer to the character.

Good actors (and why even talk of others?) commit themselves totally to revealing their most private selves. In rehearsal, bonds of trust develop that in other life situations take months, even years, to create. Now it must happen in days, weeks. Time is always limited— the clock ticks away. As the weeks go by, tempers are lost, animosities develop, tears are shed, private jokes that outsiders would never understand keep the company laughing, and friendships are fixed in life-long cement. It is more than a work relationship, much more. In the end, a family is created, and together it must now face the ultimate test of an audience.

These strangers, the outsiders, arrive, hundreds of them, to hate, to love, and to teach the company. Of course, the work goes on during performance. Good actors continue the process of discovery. They must continue to unmask, to challenge themselves. No matter the nerves, the changed heartbeat, and the excessive sweat that some experience, the actor's effort is to continue the creative work. Now, in performance, if never before, the actor realizes how dependent he is, actor to actor, upon the others; how pleased he is when he (or a colleague) gets the hoped-for big laugh; and how secretly delighted he is at the sharp burst of applause at the end of the first act. "Never mind," he says to himself, "just do the work." Yes, of course, but tonight, with the strangers out there, the risk is more real, the reward greater. It's different.

It is extraordinary, the emotional bond that can develop between actors as they live through the imaginary experiences in the performance of a play. The imaginary fighting, loving, hurting each other—that is, the highs and lows of the performance—can seem more real than real to the good actor, who always remains connected, who is always present.

Then suddenly the lights come up and the actors are wrenched back to reality, drained, sometimes exhilarated, their emotional reservoir almost empty. The depth of feeling, the unconscious resentments, the uncovered, even unnamed, responses are often hard to cope with night after night on the way home. Actors often need to have a quick drink with some of their colleagues to help them "come down" after the show.

The process of rehearsing and performing a play is a communal event different from all other similar work experiences. Different because, in what the actor is doing, there is the summoning of the sometimes-unwilling unconscious. Different because of the emotional unmasking that is sometimes necessary, and always the fear of the flop, and always in front of strangers—every night the same and every night unpredictably different. The one absolute is the need to count on, to depend on, to offer the self generously to the others. That connection is never forgotten. That dependency, that bond established as the play runs, is somewhat similar to what soldiers experience. I'm not making any invidious comparisons. For actors, their careers and creative lives depend on each other, and it can feel like life and death. From the first moment of rehearsal and throughout the run of the play, actors, like soldiers, know there must be absolute trust, confidence in, and reliance on each other's skills.

This commonality of endeavor, this empathic experiencing of each other during the weeks of rehearsing and performing, create the community. Actors sense when it's there, and they sense when it's missing. They know soon enough when they're involved in a company that has no ensemble, where there is no sense of community, and they know how painful it can be. They also know how exhilarating it can be when a company develops into a cohesive whole. A well-functioning ensemble recognizes and accepts the importance of the individual, but only insofar as it affects the whole—that is to say, there is the joy of the self, bouncing off other selves, changing other selves. And all of it is in the service of this new theatrical event that the writer has imagined and has never happened before. The desire for this community, the physical and mental pleasure that sometimes emerges, keeps the actor-artist working, even in an unresponsive theater. Unfortunately, the whole new exhilarating theatrical event has to end. Often much too soon, the closing notice goes up. It's over, and the family is dispersed, and all go to their separate careers. The loneliness returns.

Actors need work. There are many reasons an actor desperately searches for work—to eat, to construct a career, to express deeply felt, creative wants. So much of the actor's work must happen alone. But I suggest that one of the strongest internal wants is to once again be part of this larger theatrical family. At some point in my own life I began to discover, with some visceral thrill, that in fact I was part of a larger community: The Acting Profession. I'm not sure when it began. Lee Strasberg, whatever else one can argue about his contributions, certainly created for anyone who studied with him a pride in the profession and the excitement of our history. Perhaps it happened to me then. Perhaps it was when I joined Actors' Equity and got my union card. The recognition that I was a member of this five-thousand-year-old community was important, and it remains so.

SUCCESS

In every community, in every culture, there is the question of "success." What is it, when is it, how is it defined, and who defines it in our profession?

Success for an actor can mean, in a general way, recognition by one's colleagues and by the public. With it comes financial rewards and even those famous little statues. More specifically, there is critical acclaim in a particularly difficult role, which moves the career forward (no money, no little statue, however). These add up to important, meaningful, tangible success, which means, simply, getting more work, and the potential for a little less worry about next year (the worry never really stops, no matter today's acclaim).

There are other victories, though, less obvious but deeply

satisfying. If you're lucky, there may come a time when you don't have to read and audition for a part ever again. They've seen your work and they want you. That's a real blessing (even further on, way further on, when they say, "Get me a (your name here) type," because they know you wouldn't dream of taking such a small part).

Then there is the business of acting (as opposed to the art of), which has its own successes. Get a top agent to represent you. That's a big deal. Book a national commercial that gets a lot of "plays." It's a rent-payer for months. Better yet, a small part in a long-running series, replayable for years—it will send your kid to college. It is not why you chose to spend your life in the theater, but it's an element of a certain kind of success.

THE ELEGANT SOLUTION

Then, for the actor-artist, there are the more internal, private, secretly satisfying successes (as there are for every artist and committed professional in every field). There are those times when the actor, wrestling with an elusive element of a part, hits a brick wall; she knows, sees clearly, what a particular character relationship should be, but it hides, evades, will not emerge even though all around her say, "It's fine, what you are doing is fine." But she knows better. This artist never stops searching, trying, testing. Then one night, perhaps after the opening—or if she's lucky, before—she gets it. Clear, cool, simple. Often revelatory. Not necessarily recognized by anyone except her as part of a whole. That is a very real success, and sometimes it is enriched enough to change the very way of work. The quiet thrill, the internal tickle of excitement when an actor uncovers the mystery of the character's deeply buried and innermost passions must be akin to a scientist's sudden discovery of an enlightened pathway. The elegant solution, shared later over a drink with another actor who understands and has been there, is one of the triumphs that maintain our connection to the world of the theater.

SUPERSTITION

Another adhesive that keeps our community connected is our myths, our stories of once-upon-a-time, our superstitions, only half believed but nonetheless tightly held, some going back hundreds of years. Serious "dos" and serious "don'ts." You probably know that if we want to wish an actor well on opening night we say "merde" or "break a leg." If we said "good luck," the theater devils, always lurking, would hear and make the opposite happen. And please don't give flowers before the performance. And don't you dare wear blue (unless you wear silver with it!). You mustn't whistle in a theater because a stagehand will take it as a cue to remove the set. In the old days, unemployed sailors would do theatrical rigging and would communicate to each other using coded whistles to move sets up and down. An errant whistle could send scenery crashing down on someone's head. And don't you dare put your hat on the makeup table (maybe because it means you'll be leaving soon?). During a run, theaters are never "closed" because there is the fear that the show will close; we say theaters are "dark." And don't open your umbrella in the dressing room (maybe because bad weather will stop audiences from coming?). Actors never mention by name a famous play by William Shakespeare. We call it "The Scottish Play" because failure inevitably follows when you call it by its rightful name. And of course there must always be one light left on center stage, a ghostlight, or else abused and disrespected actor-ghosts will make havoc.

TRADITIONS

Then there is the recent demise of George Spelvin. His extraordinary work graced the stages of hundreds of theaters around the country for many decades, often playing in different cities on the same night, at times only a walk-on (even an animal or a corpse!). He was truly ubiquitous. He's gone now without even an obituary, as anonymous in death as he was in life. That is because, at one time, when an actor was asked to "double," to play a second part, for which he had not been specifically cast, "George (or Georgina) Spelvin" was placed in the program. Producers liked it in the playbill because it made the cast look larger. For the actor-artist, it was a chance to transform and disguise oneself so completely as not to be recognizable. Now, however, because actors are pleased to let the audience know they are playing two or even three parts, George and Georgina Spelvin have been retired, and it is the actor's versatility that is celebrated.

Then there was the time . . . in 1958, when I was hired by the Theatre Guild, holder of some of the American theater's grandest traditions, to direct, on Broadway, *Third Best Sport*, starring Celeste Holm. The production stage manager given to me was the Guild's best, Karl Nielsen. A twenty-year veteran with the Guild, and the stage manager for many of the greatest stars (Katharine Hepburn, Ruth Gordon, Tallulah Bankhead, and Rex Harrison, among many others), Karl was a great ship captain, a tough taskmaster, and, most of all, a Traditionalist. For every opening, at his desk, Karl wore a tuxedo. And Karl, every single night, at the star's first entrance, clapped his hands sharply together once, to trigger applause, just in case it was a sleepy crowd. Because entrance applause usually happened, Karl knew, even when the star insisted he or she didn't care, that it would be unnerving if it didn't come—and the stars were grateful for his concern. And it always worked (I have tried it since). I once asked Karl if "Celeste" was in her dressing room. "Miss Holm, Michael. Miss Holm is not in yet." He didn't care what I called her in private, but in his part of the world, there was a tradition to be followed. And I was glad to follow.

Chapter 4
Relaxation, Concentration, and the Breath

Actors are storytellers. The work of theater is to take the worlds of science, art, psychology, and politics and turn them into stand-up stories. It begins with the writer; that's the story part. The stand-up part is the actor. The actor bends, twists, gives birth to the language and the body of this newly conceived soul, slaps its imaginary bottom, and up stands the character. In order for the birth to be healthy, the actor's body must be available, responsive, and able to execute the most complicated ideas. And that means it must be a body without unnecessary muscular tension, a body without strain.

RELAXATION

In 1975, Herbert Benson, a professor of medicine at Harvard University, wrote *The Relaxation Response*. That book, which is primarily about the use of meditation as a tool for healthy living, describes in great and useful detail the hows and whys of muscular relaxation. An extremely important book, particularly for performers, it made people worldwide conscious of what muscular tension and muscular relaxation were. It quickly became a bestseller.

As it happens, Lee Strasberg had been teaching deep muscular relaxation and its importance to actors for years in the Actors Studio and in his private classes. Those of us who had studied with Lee laughed when the book was published, and we decided that Dr. Benson must have taken classes with Lee.

In Lee's class, we were taught that muscular tension (not nervousness, mind you) was a major enemy of the actor's ability to concentrate, as well as of unimpeded, intuitive emotional responses. All his classes began with deep total relaxation exercises, followed by exercises to develop concentration and to practice simple and then more complicated sensory tasks.

As I watched myself and others, I began to question what, in fact, caused tensed muscles beyond what was necessary to accomplish a simple task—in a word, strain. It became important for me to understand what caused strain before I tried to get rid of it.

Unnecessary tension does not occur in mammals other than humans. With slow-motion cameras we are able to see the muscularity of the cheetah going seventy-odd miles-per-hour toward the kill—without an ounce of strain: enormous use of the muscles, but only as much as necessary. Not an ounce extra. When an eagle in flight reaches down and catches the salmon in its claws, there is no strain. Tensed muscles, of course, but no strain. So why and when does a human tense muscles unnecessarily?

TENSION IN LIFE

We humans use both the relaxed and the tensed muscle as tools in our daily experiences, productively and instinctively. Tensed muscles to cut off unwanted sensation; relaxed muscles to enhance the fullness of a desired experience. If you've had a chicken in the refrigerator for five days and you're not sure whether it's edible, when you hold it to your nose, you tense every facial muscle so as to avoid the fullness of what might be unpleasant. On the other hand, if you are going to smell the roses, you relax your face before you smell, in the hopes of getting all of what will be a wonderful experience. If you've chosen to take a hot bath and want to test the water, the hand that goes into the bathtub better be a relaxed hand in order to get information quickly. Tension to suppress and relaxation to encourage the fullness of an experience. In the Civil War there was a lack of anesthesia for amputations. The best they could do was give soldiers a lead bullet and say "bite hard." Those tensed jaw muscles managed to suppress some pain.

Furthermore, the conventional crying face that we envision is not the face of crying. It's the face of trying not to cry by tensing. If we didn't want to suppress the tears, we would not tense our face muscles. On the verge of tears, the body uses tension to keep the deeply felt, internal response private; in our effort to hide inappropriate self-consciousness, we tense; in our effort to hide nervousness, we tense. And if we choose not to let our hot anger become public, we use tension to stop the heat from becoming visible. It is natural for humans to use tension in these ways, unconsciously and habitually.

The actor, however, in his work, needs exactly the opposite: the desire and the willingness to let everything move up, to cut off nothing.

RELAXATION FOR THE ACTOR

The actor wants every impulse, every emotional thrust, every quick, intuitive intellectual prompt or physical jolt to be received unimpeded, spontaneously and without judgment. Muscular tension, physical strain, is the enemy. A relaxed body—not a flaccid body—is the great encourager of character-truth, situational-truth, personal-truth. Only then, working without strain, can the actor-artist make choices about what response stays and what is excluded. Acting demands availability to sensation, to the sudden surprise, the unexpected generosity, the loving look, the delicate touch, the subtlest imaginings, and, most important, the free-flowing intuition. Tension makes barriers. The intuition doesn't shout; it whispers.

If tension is the main enemy, then the learned ability to work with a muscularly relaxed body by tensing and relaxing an isolated group of muscles is the greatest ally. Dealing physically with tension—not intellectually ("Am I tense? Am I relaxed?")—means learning to listen to your body. It will tell you, "Release! Let go!" and after a while, you will.

To become aware of strain as you work and to learn how to release it—easily, quietly, without exaggerated effort—is a learned technique that takes practice, which must continue throughout a career. It is worth the effort because experiencing for the first time the living-through of a high-end emotional scene without strain, push, or physical tension is mind-altering. It allows the actor to think more clearly, to experience more fully, to cope with nerves, and to use more completely what he has prepared to bring to the work. There is a major difference, of course, between tension and intensity. Intensity is what is required: the total commitment to a desired want under the heightened circumstances of the play. But desired intensity, the commitment to and involvement with a moment, must be accomplished without muscular tension.

Actors will correctly ask, "But suppose the character is tense?" Creative work demands that the actor, the creator of the character as written by the author, must approach the most extreme situations without actor-strain. That means creating the character's particular physicality, including the possibility of exaggerated muscular tension, if necessary. The actor's instrument must first be relaxed and the actor can then choose which specific way his character uses—allows—tension.

Great artists do not allow unnecessary tension in their work. The stratospheric leaps of Mikhail Baryshnikov and his colleagues, or Willie Mays (again, that slow-motion camera) leaping to the heavens for a baseball, are without strain. Watch closely and it will seem as if, at the peak of the leap, had they needed to go further up, they could have. No gritted teeth, no furrowed brow. Great singers hitting the highest of high Cs, seem, if necessary, able to go even higher. Strasberg and Benson were both right: Unconscious and unrequired body tension is unhealthy, and it is the enemy of the performing artist. The muscularly relaxed instrument fosters spontaneous emotional and intellectual responsiveness, and it is what encourages the major strength of the actor: the ability to concentrate.

CONCENTRATION: TO FOCUS THE ATTENTION, STAY FOCUSED, AND SHIFT THE FOCUS

Concentration demands that all of what must be accomplished in the play—the internal life, the external life, and the text—must be experienced as a series of fully realized moments, each of which needs the actor's uninterrupted attention. Concentration is what ensures that each moment is fully realized before moving on to the next moment—all while the text continues. Concentration catches and holds an audience, pinned, to the story.

Always, the actor's most important strength is the ability to concentrate, moment to moment—without forcing—on what the artistic choice demands. It means to be totally present, uncompromisingly focused, whether pouring a drink, interrogating a witness, enjoying a kiss, or slicing cheese. It is more difficult, of course, when the object or the action does not encourage total presence. Give the cheese as much attention as you give the kiss—even more, because you won't get much help from the cheese.

Unforced and relaxed concentration seems so easy in our daily lives, at least most of the time. In life, concentration can come and go with little consequence. In the theater, the concentrated moment must be accomplished, fully and completely, now. For the actor-artist, nerves, anxiety, wanting to do well, being watched, and self-judging all get in the way. But concentration is like a muscle. Use it, practice it, it gets stronger. Test it, make demands of it, and it becomes inherent. Sooner rather than later, if the actor works at it, the ability to focus, to stay focused, and then to shift the focus becomes one of the actor's most important tools. There is no important, satisfying, serious acting without concentration.

Once relaxation and concentration are achieved, the road on which all the actor's physical, emotional, and intellectual truths will travel is the actor's breath.

THE BREATH

The simple, life-giving, ongoing, never-ending cousin of the heartbeat (and great friend of the actor) is the unimpeded breath. Unimpeded. That's the key. The actor must allow the breath to do what it knows how to do and remove everything that impedes it. The breath is the road on which the actor's true voice, enriched, perhaps, with great language, travels and reaches its destination.

In life we humans tolerate much behavior that impedes breathing. We manipulate the breath inappropriately, for instance by "holding" it when we are under duress and by not exhaling it fully.

The impeded breath prevents athletes from reaching their physical potential. I've been told that Monica Seles, a famous tennis champion, understanding the value of the "exhale" during physical exertion, was the first to make those wild sounds, those grunts and squeals, in a tennis match every time she hit the ball. She said she did it to remember to release her breath. I don't suggest the actor grunt and squeal exactly, though there are times when exhaling on a sound can be a useful tension reliever, even illuminating an inner truth that is not verbalized in the text.

The impeded breath can also affect retention of information. If you sit, studying, scrunched up in a chair for an hour or two, you will find yourself reading the same sentence two or three times, trying to memorize and being unable to retain. Without thinking, you'll get up, stretch, move around, and allow the lungs to fill up. Then, when you sit down again, you'll find that you memorize more quickly and need to reread passages less often. You have been sitting with tensed muscles (including the diaphragm), which prevent oxygen from reaching the brain. By getting up and stretching, the road of the breath is reopened. Diaphragm tension impedes thinking as much as it impedes speaking. Shallow breathing is an enemy. But don't "take" a breath. Allow a breath. Remember to allow the body to do its thing. You will perform, you will fight, flee, and, yes, make love, better when you are relaxed and breathing easily.

Speaking on the unimpeded breath in the theater is the best way an actor can ensure he is heard by the audience sitting in the last row—this is commonly referred to as projection. More than that, a voice, on the breath, carries with it—whether in the theater or in front of a camera (where decibels are not important)—hidden content, subtlety. Actors must remind themselves that the breath is the road on which not only great language and even poetry ride but also the urgent voice, the colloquial voice, rich with unspoken meanings. Strengthening relaxation, concentration, and the breath is a correct concern for an actor as she develops work habits. Of course, she does not want to think about them when she is performing, except in a heightened performance moment when she becomes aware of physical tension, or that her focus is superficial, or that her breath is shallow. Then—and only then—does the learned ability to correct course become an important part of craft.

A gentle reminder. While standing in the wings, about to enter or waiting for "action," remind yourself to release the belly (leave vanity for the beach). Releasing the belly relaxes the diaphragm. Breathe easily, quietly. And very important: remind yourself to speak when the lungs are full. Many of us fill up, exhale, then speak. Speak on the breath. Let all that good stuff in you have an unobstructed road so it can be shared.

Chapter 5
The Audition

My city—New York—has always been home to some of the best actor-artists in the Western world, but even here, where there are great opportunities, it is an ongoing struggle for the actor to be seen as a mature artist. Only the very best directors and hardly ever the producers see actors as valued collaborators, worthy of serious attention and consideration, and as equal partners in the work of the theater. The general public, on the other hand, has always cared about actors, wondered at actors, in fact has always wanted to be up there in the bright lights with the actors. In the past, and for hundreds of years, little towns and big cities were excited to see us arrive with our platform and our passion, ready to shake them up (and equally relieved to see us go!). Today they pay a great deal of money—more than they should have to—to see actors do what actors do so well. Admiration, high regard, and recognition are what actors get from audiences now. Not so from the industry.

Historically, even the best producers treated actors as children, well behaved, not very bright, but useful. Until 1920, producers could and did fire actors without reason, work them endless hours, and strand them without pay on the road. It was unjust, without equity. Finally, only after the monumental Actors' Strike for a union in 1919, with great stars fighting it out on both sides, with theaters closing and money being lost, did actors win some equity in contracts. With the arrival of the Actors' Equity Association, attention was finally paid to the worth of the actor.

Even so, until the early 1950s there was still in the actor's contract the "Five-Day Clause," which gave the producer the right, for the first five rehearsal days after the contract was signed, to fire the actor for no reason, and with no recompense, simply by handing him a "pink slip" or by sending him a telegram before midnight of the fifth day.

There is a grim, dark joke that actors told each other to help them laugh at the pain, the indignities of their chosen profession. So . . .

An actor, who hasn't worked for most of the season, is cast in the best part he's had in a long time. He's living in a small room on 49th Street, near 10th avenue. On the first day—the reading—he tries hard to show them what he's capable of, and the director smiles at him. He lunches with the other actors. All's well. At the end of the second day, the director doesn't say goodnight when the actor does, but, well, he's busy talking to three of the other actors. On the third day, the producer shows up; there's much jollity with the other actors, but the producer ignores him. He eats lunch by himself. On the fourth day, there are notes for everyone . . . except him. Now he is sleepless and sweating. On the fifth, he's working badly, and he knows it. At the end of the day, he says goodnight to the stage manager and stands, waiting for the pink slip that he now expects. Nothing. "Of course," he thinks, "it'll be a telegram." He walks home. The rehearsal was at the Malin studios on 46th Street, where most Broadway shows rehearsed. As he leaves the building, he is surrounded by working actors laughing and joking. At home, it's seven o'clock. No food, just pacing, thinking over and over: "What could I have done, what didn't I do?" Now it's 11:30 . . . maybe, maybe . . . but no. At ten minutes to midnight, there's a knock on the door. "It's Western Union." Of course. Open the door. Take it. The deepest, darkest moment. The Western Union "boy" waiting, perhaps for a tip, curious. Finally, the opening . . . and then from him great whoops of joy, relief and delirium, laughing, laughing . . . And the Western Union boy says, "Great news, huh?" "YES!" he says, "MY MOTHER DIED!"

Grim, dark, funny, but somewhere in it is buried truth. The awful hurt of rejection. The desperate need for work. That five-day clause remained in the Equity contract for too many years. Only after the five days were over could the actor begin the mysterious process of creating a new human being. Because what he was doing during those first five days of torture was auditioning.

Though actors no longer have to do five days of auditioning, there are all the callbacks that make it seem to last that long. Whatever the form this auditioning takes—this offering of oneself, hoping they will buy—it is selling. Cynical, perhaps, but accurate. Some very mediocre actors are very good at it. Some brilliant actors are terrible auditioners.

Because I do not believe there is one way that fits every audition experience, what I suggest here should be examined critically, argued with, accepted, and even rejected.

In reading for a job, a part in a play, an actor understandably will be concerned with what "they" want, with what some other person tells you "they" are looking for. And the actor will wonder, "What will read?" and will practice "speaking the speech," and repeat at the auditions what was practiced the night before—presenting to them what one hopes "they" are looking for. I say, "STOP!"

All that is a talent killer. Even when they don't know it, they are auditioning you, the deepest, most committed, most present you: your talent, your chops, your specialness. The most important element of this uncovering is that you forget about them, and aggressively. The hell with them! It is by your choices, by your approach, by your willingness to go all the way in pursuit of your idea that they see the character in greater dimension. Here, then, are some suggestions.

At home, read carefully with all your good insight the given circumstances. If you only have a few pages, and they tell you nothing of the backstory, make it up from what you have. Make a choice about the one, most important thing you want and what you're going to do about getting it. Let the text emerge out of the want. Resist repeating line readings. As you respond to what you sense in the text, choose one, single strongest want in the little moment or two they offer you (including the "Hellos"). Let them have you, immersed in the story. Give them you, unzipped (figuratively, please). Trust your talent and be willing to go all the way in pursuit of your choice, even if it is what they consider to be "wrong" for the part. If you have truly revealed yourself to them, they will be interested in you, and at the very least they will give you a direction: "No, not that way; do it *this* way."

All auditions, whether prepared for days or only for a few hours, should always be an improvisation, spontaneous, happening for the first time, full of surprises, as all improvisations are—even as you stay with the text, word for word. The auditioner surprised is the auditioner interested. And when they call you back, don't repeat. Go further. If it's a comedy, find a deadly serious moment. And if it's a serious play, find a small laugh somewhere. It must be full of what only you would bring to it.

When the casting people and directors (good ones, anyway) watch ten or twenty actors reading the same three pages for hours on end, what are they looking for? They want to see a real, living, non-acting person, relaxed and pleased to be there. They want to be jiggled awake by some simple, revealed truth. Remember: they are not auditioning the material; they are auditioning you. They want to see that you're more than what's written; they want at least a moment of you, totally present. Stop selling. You are not a product.

And if they don't buy? Fuck 'em! Cursing is useful in overcoming the desperate desire to get work.

There is, of course, another side to the audition process. It gives the casting, directing, and producing fraternity an opportunity to meet previously unknown actors. Make sure they see you at the top of your game—living truthfully in an imaginary world. Notice, I don't say "performing in," not even "acting in." "Living fully present" in that world. Even more reason, therefore, that you stay loose, free-flowing, uncaring, a talent with whom these employers want to work—if not in this play, then in another.

Actors have discovered that their best auditions are those in which the actor doesn't really care whether he's cast or not. Move yourself to that place. You are good at creating "lies like truth." The truth is that getting the job won't change your life; you are more than this part. And even if you don't believe it, it helps to make the effort.

Another thing. Take a cab (with your last dollars, you deserve it) to an important audition, and in the cab, play "the imaging game." Really, try it even as you laugh at it. "Image" the receptionist happy to see you. See the auditioners rise as you enter, pleased you came.

Then see yourself working brilliantly, the best ever. Perhaps they'll applaud when you finish. Seriously, if you don't do this, your mind will not be empty. It will be filled with worry, with negative, dark concerns—as it is with all actors. Instead, when you arrive and sit, waiting to be called, stay away from how you will use the text and stay with imaging that will amuse you. When you walk into the room, imaging will ensure that you are really looking at them. It will encourage paying attention to the reader, to the people behind the table.

Of course you'll be nervous. You care. Don't hide it. Remember to breathe. Pursue the task, the want you set for yourself. Trust your talent. Enjoy the challenge.

II.

In Rehearsal

Chapter 6
Confronting the Character

The beginning of a discussion of rehearsal must be the actual beginning: getting the job. We can't skip over that moment, those thirty seconds after you've been told, "You have the job. The part is yours." It's a glorious moment of genesis, of a beginning. You are working. You are wanted. Not merely a general you, but the craft-you, the artist-you, is wanted. Of course, I'm speaking now of a phone call about a decent part in a stimulating play, but even a commercial is a rent payer and should be celebrated. That phone call, even for a big-name actor when it's a project he really wants, has the same "kick," the same updraft of fulfillment. The most craft-worthy, most private, and most vulnerable artist that you can offer is what's wanted. Celebrate the phone call (or the email). Even if you insist on waiting for the contract to be signed before alerting the world, pour a drink, buy a new shirt.

Getting the job is the high point. Then the work begins. And no matter whether it becomes what the actor had hoped for or is painfully devoid of creative exploration, he will do the work. The actor must struggle, sometimes against mediocrity; most times, it is to be hoped, he is thrilled by collaborative creativity.

Every actor knows that each new project offers a new experience, new challenges, new solutions. The past is the past. Now, there are only questions: "Can I do it? Will I find a way? Will I fail or succeed?" How fortunate to live a life without a moment of boredom!

THE FIRST DAYS

If the work is a revival, a Shakespeare or Tennessee Williams play, put aside the remembered performances, the brilliant, critical essays, and the readily available YouTube videos. Don't contaminate those first moments of you, the text, and, most important, the other actors. You have already read and thought about this wonderful play and your character. What is now new and exciting are these surprising people, these actor-characters you are meeting for the first time. Be present with them. Make these first days more about them than about you.

Even in a new play, when you are asked to give life to a human being who has never before stood up in the world three-dimensionally, open yourself wide eyed to the others, without judging the world unfolding around you, even before you concern yourself with the specificity of your own character.

HAMLET'S HAT

Soon you will inevitably be led to the face-to-face confrontation with the on-the-page character you will inhabit. These beginning moments, these first questings, are very evocative. No answers, only questions. No matter how provocative, how stimulating this new entity, it is still two-dimensional, lying there on the page. What it can become is fluid, changeable; it is essentially undiscovered. As the actor begins to work, this figment—shadowy, hooded—coming from the writer's imagination and igniting yours, begins to move off the page until character and actor stand facing each other.

Still separate, they are strangers, unsure, hopeful, wary, eager to find affinities, connections. Think of Richard Burbage, Shakespeare's leading actor, meeting Hamlet for the first time. There was no learned criticism, no deconstruction, no post-modernism. Just Burbage and Hamlet. What a meeting that must have been!

Now begins the extraordinary challenge inherent in the art of acting: the need for two to become one. It is neither all the one, nor all the other. It is finding the self in the character and the character in the self. During the next weeks, the more mentally muscular the questionings, the more the hidden internal landscapes will shift from cloudy storm to sudden sunlight, the more the author and the text will be revealed.

It's like a dance, one moment breathtakingly in harmony, the next, apart, unconnected. The character makes demands, insists. The actor bends, resists. The two face each other as equals. The actor, in effect, has an argument with the character as if it were a real, three-dimensional person. If I were to give each a voice, you would hear the character turn to the author and say of the actor, "Him? HIM!? He's not smart enough, pretty enough, tough enough, anything enough!" And the actor turns to the director and says, "Damn, why does he . . . ? He wouldn't . . . He shouldn't! I can't believe he . . . !" Best that the author and director stand mute at this point.

Of course, the actor knows that the primary responsibility is his; he is the one who will bring the two into one. The character doesn't easily reveal secrets or core truths to the actor. These come slowly as the two probe and push, making a little opening here, a sudden unmasking there. Both must be pliable. The actor says, "I see how strongly you feel about that, but you must give me room to encourage the incorrect, the probably-wrong-but-spontaneous impulses that occur to me." At times, the character will be adamant: "This is the way it must be. I've seen you try different ways to accomplish this. I've let you explore, but it must be the way I want it." Both must give up a piece of themselves.

Finally, the differences, at least the important ones, become reconciled, and this new entity, this stand-alone piece of humanity, this never-before-seen Hamlet, this Hedda, emerges. Yes, never before seen.

If it's an important Hamlet, a challenging Hamlet, it must be the actor's Hamlet, the actor's Willy Loman, the actor's Hedda Gabler; it can no longer be the writer's. The playwright may hate or love who her creature has become, but it now belongs to the actor. Playwrights understand this and look forward to being surprised—happily, they hope. That's what the theater is: a collaboration. That's why when we go to see a new production of a play we've seen many times, we are excited, anticipatory, hoping it won't be the same-old same-old. We want revelation. We never know who will be wearing Hamlet's hat.

TOOLS OF DISCOVERY

To bring about this creative joining of actor and character, what must the actor bring to this search? What tools, what pieces of herself must—not might, but must—the actor-artist bring to this journey, which ends in inhabiting another human being? Here is what I feel most centrally.

GENEROSITY

Offer yourself without restraint. Reject preconceptions. Go anywhere the character wants you to travel. Risk. Go too far. Be wrong, gloriously wrong. Offer the whole self—the heroic, the shameful, the hidden pieces—that the role and the play demand. And use your whole body—not just your mind and your mouth, but your neck, your crossed leg, the way you sit and stand, walk and run. Oh, yes, and allow your ego to be changed: enlarged, shrunk, wounded.

CURIOSITY

Become interested in every hinted and suggested relationship, every surprising verb or unusual adjective in the text. Pay attention to place descriptions that are presumably there just for the designer, but which are also useful for the actor (but ignore needless stage directions: "She sits," "He crosses upstage," "She cries," and so on). Read the character as you would a really good detective story, with you as the detective. And look to be surprised.

CONFIDENCE

A good actor recognizes the enormous value of "I don't know," instead of "I'm supposed to know." The very nature of acting takes pleasure in not knowing how or when the best answers will unfold and reveal themselves. Confidence (and experience) gives the actor the excitement of moving forward, even when he does not yet see clearly the most illuminated answers. Confidence says, "Trust the other actors, trust the text, trust your imagination, and trust your craft." You will discover what choice must be discarded and what must be pursued. Enjoy the ups and downs of the journey. Come to play.

AGGRESSION AND PATIENCE

Aggression is not violent. Patience is never passive. Aggression and patience together mean that actors, without certainty, without even an end view, will be willing to move forward assertively while also allowing for a relationship to develop in its own way. Push that famous envelope, dare failure, don't be concerned with "Is it right?" And remember to leave air, remember to breathe. Be patient.

Flora Roberts, a highly regarded play agent (and my representative as a director), told me that she began her career as an assistant to Kermit Bloomgarden while he was producing Arthur Miller's *Death of a Salesman*, starring Lee J. Cobb and directed by Elia Kazan. For three and a half weeks, Bloomgarden saw nothing from Cobb—only mumbling, head down, shrouded glances; sometimes, for a moment, a lightning flash, then nothing. Day after day. The out-of-town tryout in Philadelphia was approaching, and there was actually talk of replacing Cobb. With trepidation, the company arrived in Philadelphia to confront its first audience—and its patience was rewarded. That first night in Philadelphia, when the house lights dimmed and the stage lights came up on Jo Mielziner's evocative set, Willy Loman walked out fully materialized. I am not suggesting this as a good way of working. For years, Kazan and Cobb had worked together closely, day and night, in the Group Theatre—studying the actor's process and putting into practice new ways of creating theater—so both of them could take advantage of their long relationship that allowed for continued internal exploration.

EMPATHY

This is perhaps most important. For actors, it is the core element of their work, insofar as they need to encourage within themselves involvement with and even love of the character they're playing. The empathic response is exactly what the actor does. He nurtures that part of himself that tries to understand and embrace the peculiarities of another human being. Actor empathy brings with it (as in life) an interest in others and deepens understanding within relationships. The opposite of empathy is a kind of narcissism, self-involvement rather than involvement with the other.

Good actors know they must not only understand but also care about the person they're playing. This idea is particularly important when playing villains. An actor playing Iago asks himself, "Why it is so necessary to destroy Othello?" What is it that creates that pleasure, that satisfaction, that ferocious need? There is no need to admire, but the actor must begin to "get" what Iago gets from his evil-doing and thereby be able to dig within himself and find the little bit of Iago hiding there. Empathy helps the actor begin to experience what impels the character.

A better example: in *Richard III*, playing a fully rounded Gloucester, whose every moment is directed at becoming king, demands that the actor understand what it was like to have been born . . .

Deform'd, unfinish'd, sent before my time
Into this breathing world, scarce half made up,
And that so lamely and unfashionable
That dogs bark at me as I halt by them . . .
(*Richard III*, Act I, Scene 1, 20–23)

As the actor buries himself in what the first years of Gloucester's life were like in that still primitive culture, he begins to question whether perhaps his mother and the court threw him aside, crippled and deformed as he was. Did his brothers ridicule, tease, and abuse him? Exploring those beginnings—and even improvising with other actors on those previous events—helps the actor not only understand intellectually the outrageousness of Gloucester's behavior— his ambition and his need for revenge—but also begin to experience internally elements of his world. There are many ways to approach the character of Gloucester. What I am suggesting is one possible approach.

Insightful, provocative, and stimulating questions are more valuable than superficial answers that shut down exploration. Actors do not need to be correct, or to explain and justify their understanding of the character. They need only that sometimes very private, very secret ignition switch that deeply connects the character to the actor and which impels action.

Heroes as well as villains need the same kind of empathic research. Always concerned with both sides of the coin, the actor needs to include some aspect of the unheroic when playing the hero. Shakespeare, in one of his greatest heroes, Henry V, gives us first the Prince—drunk, disorderly, thieving, womanizing, and finally disloyal—before Hal becomes that generous, sensitive, loving commanding officer and king. Not every writer will be so helpful, and in that case the actor must create both personality sides for himself. The core of the actor's work demands objective, intellectual clarity. It also demands sympathetic understanding and compassion: empathy.

THE ELUSIVE CHARACTER

At last, the character and actor are in step, walking together, becoming one. Then suddenly there is an obstacle, a roadblock: The actor discovers—however deeply anchored he is in what the writer has given—differences between himself and the character—differences that are not getting resolved in rehearsal. What is to be done when aspects of the character remain elusive?

I suggest you welcome these differences. Rather than trying to reorganize your thinking, accept these differences and allow the character to feel the same split you feel. Allow the ambivalence of the actor to become the ambivalence of the character, even when that ambivalence seems not to be written. The differences between the two need not distance the actor from the character. The internal argument between actor and character often enriches the situation given by the playwright and can lead to behavior that is unconventional and both actor-truthful and character-truthful. In life, we often do something to which we are uncommitted and about which we have doubts—and then discover in the doing the rightness of the result. So reject overintellectualizing. Do what the character is doing and allow the actor-doubts. By allowing the differences, certainly in a rehearsal and even in a performance, the actor brings more weight, more thickness, and more subtlety to what may otherwise be superficial.

EVERYTHING THAT HAPPENS TO THE ACTOR IS HAPPENING TO THE CHARACTER

The character/actor schism is just one of many craft dilemmas that seem difficult to resolve. A way out lies in a deeply held concept: that what is happening to the actor at every moment is, in fact, what is happening to the character. One brain, one thought, one voice. For example, should the actor forget a line of text, that experience is also happening to the character—just as in life when we can't remember what we were about to say. Don't hide. When the actor is annoyed with the way she has played a moment, it is the character who doesn't like how she behaved—just as in life, when we are not pleased with our response. If the prop isn't where it's supposed to be, it is the character who can't find his keys. When one actor sees another actor in the scene playing a whole new moment, it is the character who sees his wife (for instance) never behaving like this before. Notice it. Enjoy it. Make it part of the performance. It is what "moment to moment" work means in the theater.

And then there are times when, reading the script, the actor is surprised at the reaction of the character. Her response—as she reads—is totally different from the character's, and the actor finds it unacceptable. In such situations, it would seem logical to find ways to resolve intellectually the schism that exists between the actor and the character. But often there is another way. It is not necessary to "choose" and have only one response: accept, even encourage, the major differences in response between character and actor and allow the dilemmas to become resolved in the course of rehearsal. How much better, how much more artful, it is to allow the written character to experience a wider range of responses.

It is true, of course, that in rehearsal as well as in performance, the emphasis on trusting one's own response to the play's circumstances carries certain dangers. Chief among them is the mistaken idea—for instance—that one's own embedded jealousy is enough for whatever jealousy exists in the play. The truth for which one is searching may well begin with one's own small but deeply felt pleasures or painful resentments and jealousies. They must, really, begin there. If one is to play Othello, the painful jealousy that most of us might understand must be transformed into a dreadful soul-destroying jealousy. This is not a matter of size, sound, or fury; it's about the depth of Othello's pain, the largeness of the loss that Desdemona could love someone else—and his inability to survive without her. But if the actor is to play Cassius in Julius Caesar, he dare not bring the character down to his own level, to the envy and ambition that he, the actor, is comfortable with. Rather he must encourage himself to dig down to those hidden, barely recognized responses until he sees himself as capable as Cassius of murderous conspiracy.

This searching for and finding previously unknown dark places in order to satisfy what the play demands as well as one's own artistic vision is one of the most profound experiences an actor working on a character can have. Actors are continually surprised at the new "selves" they discover in play after play, character after character. Actors can spend years unearthing different selves and learning how to access them. It is by paying deep attention to the given circumstances of the text that the actor can discover which "self" to bring to work.

Chapter 7
The Partner

To look is not to see;
To see is not to have vision.
To have vision is to see beyond seeing,
Bringing a torch to that which has been hidden.

I wrote this for myself as an experiment to see if I could state simply, specifically, and economically the need for a concentrated, multilayered relationship to the partner. There are many variations on this relationship, many influences that change that way of seeing, but for the actor, at the root of the theater is the need for, and the total attention paid to, the Other.

In the theater of the Greeks 2,500 years ago, there was a time when only the poet himself spoke the text, aided by the chorus, which danced, sang, and responded to him. Then one day the first of the great Athenian tragedians, Aeschylus, decided, "I need someone else, someone to argue with," and there it was: an actor, the first partner. From there, Aeschylus's successor Sophocles decided he needed yet another actor, and so began our profession.

There is nothing more important, as these partners face each other, than that each wants to affect the other. No matter that it seems to the audience that the actor is just ruminating; no matter that it seems primarily about the great pleasure available in language, as in Mercutio's "Queen Mab" speech in *Romeo and Juliet*. The actor must choose how and why she wants to affect her partner. "How will I change him? What can I do to make him bend my way?" Obviously, the only way an actor will know that the partner is being affected, is changing, is by paying close attention specifically to every breath change, every blink, every hinted positive and negative response.

Just as important as "doing to" is "receiving from" the partner. Receiving wants a relaxed, non-acting, concentrated openness to everything, play related or not. Not just looking at but *seeing* the partner. Hearing with the eyes; seeing with the ears. Lear says to the blind Gloucester, "Look with thine ears" (Act IV, Scene 6). One might also say to a deaf man, "Listen with thine eyes." Both are excellent advice to actors.

I have always been uncomfortable with the admonition, "Look at your partner when you talk to her!" It's too simplistic, mechanistic. Perhaps sometimes, yes, look at her, but no rules, please. The only absolute is the importance of the other.

It's not as easy as it may sound. Actors are properly involved with what they want, how to get it, the strength of their convictions, the depth of their responses. But no matter the inner life, the active task is to give all your attention to the partner. Make him—not you—the most important person in the scene. As you notice how he is responding, listen, not only to what he says but also to the sound of it—the pauses, the breath, the tempo. Listen so that you hear with your inner ear. Notice, as he speaks, body language that reveals or conceals. You will get the surface connotations via the text easily and quickly; it's the subtler things you want to be available to receive. Ask of yourself only that your body be relaxed and your breath constant, quiet, and easy. No matter the scene, forget about "being" anything—upset, angry, confused, all the things that are results and which happen on their own. There can be enormous rewards.

You will say, "But that's what I do in life. No matter how I'm feeling, I hear; I often suspect something below the words." Yes. Exactly. How many times have we said, in the face of indignant denials from a friend, "You're angry, aren't you?" We caught something. We sensed something. Humans have learned to "read" the Other, irrespective of the words. We have also learned over millennia that we acquire life-saving information through the five senses that bypasses the rational brain and leads to immediate action. "I don't know why, but I suddenly . . ." "I had this strange feeling . . ." "There is something about that place that . . ." "I can't explain it, but I just don't trust her . . ." More than in most professions, actors must develop—through practice—an instrument that is highly attuned to the unspoken, the hidden, and be always "tuned in" to the partner.

There is general concern today about how exciting technology is changing the way people relate to each other. From earliest childhood now, the eyes are buried in handheld devices. The gathering of information face to face has become unpracticed. The subtleties of the voice are lost to texting. It is a serious concern, particularly for actors whose skills come from the ability to read faces, to hear vocal nuance, and to experience the Other's physical presence. More than ever, the actor must train himself to notice the partner's warm hand, the tightening of the lips, the sharpness of the tone of voice. Noticing means recognizing that there is something different in the partner, something unexpected, seemingly unimportant, or otherwise half-hidden. There is great pleasure in suddenly catching an inference, an unexpected subtext of which even the actor/character had been unaware. It can change a relationship. Sometimes it can happen that, after playing the same moment for weeks, something erupts that was always there but had until then gone unnoticed.

For my final audition in 1949 for the Actors Studio (in front of Kazan, Strasberg, and Cheryl Crawford!), I did a scene from *Home of the Brave* by Arthur Laurents. In the play, a sergeant (played by my friend, Bernard Kates) who had helped my character recover from a battle-fatigue breakdown quoted a poem to me, which included the line, "Coward, take my coward's hand." Later in the play, in order to get the sergeant (who has by now lost an arm) to accept my help with his gear, I remind him of the line from the poem, "Coward, take my coward's hand." He smiles, accepts my help, and in a moment the play is over. Bernard and I rehearsed this scene for many weeks, saying those lines to each other over and over. At the audition, working rather well, we suddenly, and at the same moment, heard something neither of us had heard before. For the first time, instead of "Coward, take my coward's hand," we heard, "Coward, take MIKE HOWARD'S hand." "Mike Howard"—my own name!—instead of "my coward." We stopped. We stared at each other. We began to laugh. We hugged. And we exited full of the extraordinariness of the moment, not giving a damn whether we passed the audition or not, immersed only in our small miracle. A week later we learned we were both accepted. Then we cared.

Why was it that in all those weeks we never heard it? I suggest that the adrenaline, the high, comes when the actor is relaxed and concentrated. In a performance, every nerve is more alive. Hearing is heightened, seeing is sharpened. Toward the end of the audition, Barney and I were working extremely well, zoned in on each other, both of us fully concentrated on the partner. Only then were we able to hear what had been unheard.

Chapter 8
The Relationship between
Actor and Director . . . and Writer

It would be foolish to try to generalize about two imaginary theater professionals, actor and director, doing an imaginary project, but there are some concepts about this relationship that can be examined and emphasized. The relationship is important because once the contract is signed, the actor-director connection is going to influence deeply the next months of the actor's life. How should one approach it? Generously. Optimistically. Put self-protective armor aside (although you may need it later). Remember: the director cast you; he wanted you. *You.*

Do not expect the director to say and do the things that other directors you've liked have said and done. Be interested and be accepting. Assume always that the director will have a concept and ideas that are challenging and different from your own. Be curious.

In the best of circumstances, the director will lay the groundwork for a creative community. She will share her view of what will unite all these disparate talents in the service of the playwright. The director is an enabler, a put-it-together-er. Casting, they will tell you, is three-quarters of the work. The director needs a concept, an overall view, a clarity about what's in the writer's gut that impelled the creation of the play, and a way to share with each actor individually what that thrust is. But when the lights go up, the director is nowhere to be seen. Only the writer and the actor are up there for the audience to love or to "take arms against." (As a director, I can tell you, it doesn't feel that way. It always felt like my blood was being spilled up there, even though, at times, I was in the bar next door.)

In the first rehearsals, at the start of each day, the best directors understand it is necessary to create a space in which the actors feel their creative impulses are wanted, that they are here to play, to risk, to be free to do their work. Those first few days will not be too detailed, nothing will be absolute. But there will be a direction, and it will leave a lot of air in which actors can thrive. A director must in a short period of time create, out of a group of strangers—each of whom has his own agenda, ways of working, his own likes and dislikes—a cohesive whole, a community. Help him. Remain hopeful. Bring to work that part of you that is excitable, capable of being stimulated. Leave wariness at home with your self-doubts. Work unmasked.

STANISLAVSKI AND THE CREATIVE COMMUNITY

Konstantin Stanislavski, at one point in his ever-changing thinking, suggested that the best way to begin rehearsals was to have the play read to the company, perhaps by the author or artistic director. Yes! Think of being present when Chekhov read *Uncle Vanya* to the entire company, or when Stanislavski (a brilliant actor himself) read *The Lower Depths*, because Gorky may not have been available. (Or when Tennessee Williams, for that matter, read *Streetcar*.) And if we really are going to play this game, how about a day in the universe when

Shakespeare called the company (he had one) together to hear "a new thing I've done. It's called *Hamlet*"?

Of course, K.S. (as he was known in his world) was speaking of a very different theater world than the one in which most of us live. He created a theater company with actors, designers, and technicians working in their own Moscow Art Theatre building. There was no time limit, no clock ticking. There was only the time a particular work needed; some needed more time, some less. When an audience was necessary for the work to continue, they "opened." Often they rehearsed for many months.

What were they doing for all that time? Many Russian actors and directors who were there in those rehearsals have written good and important books that make fascinating and valuable reading, full of each individual's understanding (*Stanislavsky* [sic] *Directs*, by Nikolai M. Gorchakov, and *Stanislavski in Rehearsal*, by Vasily Osipovich Toporkov, among many others). Read them. They will confound, illuminate, confuse, excite, annoy, and delight the reader. They're what the actor-artist needs to keep from becoming an ideologue, a dogmatist, a know-it-all.

With a good and important playwright, here are two major elements of the early rehearsal period that Stanislavski developed, which a contemporary director, even in our hurry-up world, might find useful.

First, the deepest continuing investigation of the text—not only of simple meanings but also of the author's deepest needs in writing this play, his particular voice, the culture of his written world, the unspoken, the hinted. The actor wants to discover where and how the author's world differs from and is also the same as his own. Stanislavski wanted his actors to remain open to the physical and emotional responses that can arrive unexpected when the actors read

71

the play together many times, unconcerned with how to speak the text, with making decisions, unconcerned with how to "act." Staying open, staying available, can give the actor a veritable book of internal resources from which finally to make character choices.

Of course, so much time "at the table" is not possible in our commercial world. Actors today must delve into the text during sleepless nights, by going to libraries, even museums, by researching when it's slow at their day job behind the bar, or by using the Internet. Of course, important investigation of the text takes place through listening again and again to the other actors as they develop, ask questions, and change. Not every text will require such excavation. Not every play deserves it. A reminder: it is not answers one is looking for, only stimulating, provocative questions to research, on your feet, as you put down the script and allow your body and intuition to take hold in the weeks that follow those first readings.

Second, Stanislavski developed the concept of improvisation. Not improv for an audience as a form of entertainment but improvisation as a rehearsal tool. Improvisation, which is useful to experience the written situation with one's own language and impulses, is even more valuable as a tool to construct and live through situations that are unwritten but still suggested before and even during the life of the play. Painters have painted Othello telling stories to Desdemona and her father; why not let the actor playing Othello experience it? How valuable it would be to allow Hamlet and Ophelia to play together, to have secrets, before he heads off to college.

THE ACTOR AS EVENT DETECTIVE

When the actor begins to offer himself to the material—which is what the actor does, or should do—there is nothing more important than for him to discover the reason why the author wrote this play. (I am now talking about the artist-writer, not the writer who has to crank one out for primetime every week. I am discussing the writer who has something on her mind that needs to be heard, needs to be expressed, and this writer chooses to do it in the form of a play.)

The actor must now ask, "What is it that's burning the writer? What is it that the playwright *must* express, develop, explore, devolve?" Certainly the director *must* do exactly that, but so should the actor. Inevitably, each creative person will define for himself Tennessee Williams's need to write *Streetcar*, Miller's to write *Salesman*, Shepard's to write *A Lie of the Mind*. What is at the root for the writer? The *how* is always to tell a good story, to make it clear, to involve the audience, to affect them. But the *what* is what's hard to get at. And because we directors and actors are not scholars, we don't need absolutes or an agreement about what's correct. What we do need is to discover the writer through our lens and through the deepest reading of the text. We need to understand him and the event that he writes. That is the "what" of the author: the event.

In the play, and in any scene, the actor wants to discover why the writer has chosen to spend five, six, seven minutes of valuable storytelling time on this particular event. What is it that the writer here wants to investigate, wants to clarify? Is it the situation he's trying to move forward? Is it furthering and exploring the relationship? Or is this scene primarily about developing character? One might argue that all of these things are important. Yes, but there is one particular, specific event that the writer has decided to explore in that scene. This question of the event is not answered by reciting the plot; it's not about the plot. It's something beyond the plot that the writer cares about.

What is it, then? I can only describe it by saying that the event is the exploration of a particular kind of human experience for which the story is the chosen example; it's a specific human experience that the author is grappling with. The writer is using the story (the plot), the specific, detailed relationships, and the characters to illuminate a deeper, universal truth about our world. The more specific that truth, the more universal its application.

TODAY'S HURRY-UP WORLD

The theatrical world today bears little resemblance to that of Stanislavski's Moscow Art Theatre. Commercial theater is bound by real estate, money (or, rather, the lack of it), time constraints, and numerous other conflicts. On that first day of rehearsal, the director or the author will not read the play to you. No, all of you strangers will read it to each other. That's exciting. There is something artistically valuable and challenging, on the first rehearsal day, of walking into a room of strangers, your heart beating, and beginning to read the play, which you may not have read before. Incidentally, today's actors should feel lucky they are given the entire script on the first day of rehearsals. It used to be that actors were merely given "sides"—by which I don't mean the few scenes given in advance for the purposes of the audition. No, sides used to be all of an actor's lines, typed up by scene, with a three-word cue of when to start speaking. That was what an actor was handed when he did a play on Broadway. The producers thought actors didn't even need the whole script!

On that first day, you'll find out how good the play is and what good actors (most) of these strangers are as you begin that four-to-six-week journey, that hurry-up, don't-waste-time, time-is-money-but-we-must-have-art journey. Spontaneity, new relationships, and edgy uncertainty can feed the creative impulse—overcoming unexpected obstacles makes art. Of course, if one were lucky enough to be asked to join a permanent company, a stay-together, live-together, work-together company, year after year, it may well be that the same faces, the same feuds, the same ways of working, play after play, may not always be the best road to enriched play-making.

In the theatrical world the American actor inhabits today, there are dangers in those first days of a new company. There is always a stopwatch running, and the actor, wanting only to do the best work he is capable of, cannot help but feel the need to reassure the director, to produce visible results quickly. In such a world, it is understandable that the actor, beginning to work on a new part with a new director and new colleagues, might be seduced (or perhaps seduce himself) into quick, effective, but superficial choices, wanting to prove himself, trying to get it right, to feel it necessary to always have answers for recurring questions—rather than the stimulating "I don't know."

It is natural, it is understandable, and finally it is unproductive. It is exactly that impulse which is the obstacle to the most creative work to which good actors aspire. So give it up. Fight it. Stay within yourself. Follow internal, quirky impulses. Be wrong. Laugh at yourself. Perhaps the best, most powerful advice after the first important immersion into the text is to make the rehearsal about the others; watch them, listen to them, even test and challenge them, but do so generously. Don't be judgmental. Don't make decisions. Recognize that from the moment you read the play, your actor-self will be churning up connections, stirring the pot, when you're awake and while you sleep, and mostly unbeknownst to you. Leave it—leave yourself—alone. Make it all about the others and let what they do, say, hide, or reveal resonate with the most wide-open, available you. Trust that you will know when to begin to make choices, to begin to affect the others. Time, and the many choices attempted and rejected in rehearsal, will reveal to you when and how to achieve the strongest wants that the play, and the character, demand.

THE WORST-CASE SCENARIO

Unfortunately, the rehearsal process doesn't always allow for such valuable exploration. The actor-director relationship may not always encourage a collaboration the way Stanislavski envisioned it. So let's talk about the worst-case scenarios. In the beginning rehearsals, one director may want the actors to perform, to ACT. Another may want the actors on their feet, blocking, almost immediately. Another may want them to sit at the table for a week without any real leadership, even though the actors are ready to start moving in this particular play.

It's best that the actor not live in the safe place of hating it, of knowing better. Instead, allow the discomfort of doing completely what the director is asking. Resist the impulse to resist. Go all the way with a sense of play, even if you perceive his request as annoyingly unproductive. Particularly in the beginning of the creative process, one needs nonjudgmental play. So, even within the director's strictures, play—loosen up—improvise. You will remember that the best work between actors and the director is collaborative, on your feet, accepting, rejecting, testing.

Now, suppose in this worst-case scenario that this director continues to want not only performance on the second and third days, but he wants it exactly as he first envisioned it. If the actors are able to do it, chances are he'll want them to repeat it that way, day after day. It's annoying; worse, it's insulting. It wastes time, time the actor needs to explore the situational landscape and the complex relationships in order to give the play the best of herself.

Don't talk about it. Don't complain about it. Don't waste creative energies denying him. I suggest that the actor do exactly what the director wants (you may even find you like some of it!). Let him know how right he was to cast you. This will help reduce his anxiety and perhaps his insecurity. Do it his way a few times. It's a waste, but do it. Then, as soon as you think he no longer needs reassurance, talk to him. Tell him you now need some rehearsal time to explore other avenues, other ways of playing, other elements of the relationship. Promise him you can always go back to what he liked in the first place, that it won't be lost. Tell him you need "actor" time to be able to do what he wants, fully and richly. Hope that he will say "okay," however reluctantly, and hope that you will be able to discover elements of character and relationship that will surprise—and in spite of himself—please him. You will be concerned about wasting precious time and energy. But this is better by far than fuming and fencing for days on end without speaking to him.

Now, suppose that no matter what interesting things the actor begins to find, the director sees nothing, hears nothing, wants only his first conventional choice. No matter what good and creative responses are discovered, he wants to go back to his original, conventional idea.

I often give my students a ridiculous hypothetical scenario: If you're playing Hamlet, and the director wants you to keep your hand on your head all during "To be or not to be" for some ridiculous reason, just keep your hand on your head. Don't discuss it. Put your hand on your head, do the work of creating that extraordinary moment, and do it as well as you can—after all "To be or not to be" is not about where you put your hands. When you've done it two or three times, and he still doesn't realize the stupidity of such an idea, and when no reasonable or unreasonable discussion can shake him—then, actors, it is time to quit. Or be fired. At a certain point artistic compromise should be out of the question. When the curtain goes up, you are the one up there.

Make no mistake: creative disagreements are inevitable and necessary and, in fact, useful. The back and forth, the give and take, the willingness to accept and the refusal to give ground, are all part of the excitement of the creative process. Even the occasional bloodletting can lead to the most unexpected and valuable artistic result. So be generous. A good actor can play a moment many ways and play it well even if it isn't the actor's first choice. If you argue over every little moment, you will lose the important battle. So pick your fights.

In the end, I reject the idea that the actor's job is to be a good soldier and do whatever is asked of her, no matter how violated she feels. When generosity and availability fail, fighting for oneself and for one's artistic vision can get the actor fired. She should be willing for that to happen. I read one day in the *New York Times* that Harold Clurman and the producers of a play he was hired to direct had artistic differences and that Mr. Clurman was leaving. The next day, in a letter to the editor, Clurman said, "I had no artistic differences. I was fired." No fancy words. He did what he wanted to do; they didn't like it and fired him. Bravo, Harold!

What Harold Clurman always understood was the pleasure in and the creative value of the ensemble. It was true in the Group

Theatre experience and beyond it, just as it was true in Stanislavski's Moscow Art Theatre. The same pleasures that come from playing in a jazz trio or a classical quartet, or the beauty of executing a difficult double play in baseball, also exist for the actor in a good rehearsal. The actor wants that kind of collaborative adventure.

Chapter 9
Action, Obstacle, Immediacy

Of all the mysterious elements that create the most profound acting performance, there are three overall principles that are always present in the construction of a role: action, obstacle, immediacy.

THE DOABLE ACTION

First, perhaps most important and most simply: acting is doing. Doing with language, doing with your body, doing because there is something important that the character wants, must have. Feeling is a result—a result of preparation, of choices related to situation, character, and relationships. An actor's emotional responsiveness also develops from what he brings to the first day of rehearsal: his nervous system, his temperament, his sensitivity. The emotional response is also in reaction to what the other actors are bringing. In addition, feelings are a result of wanting, of needing something deeply and doing something about getting it. Feelings emerge on their own, when the actor is muscularly relaxed, concentrated, and deeply immersed in the event of the moment—his own or the play's. All this should result in physically and emotionally logical behavior. Good acting encourages the actor to devise doable actions that express and finally help achieve the most deeply felt emotional needs.

The text is the writer's tool. Everything the writer wants the character to reveal (or even to hide) is in the text. No matter how explicit, how revelatory, how brilliantly stated the writer's words may be, simply speaking them with intellectual clarity and eloquence is not enough. Speaking the text must come from wanting, an important want, a life-changing want. Within that text is an action, and a writer who gives you exciting, lyrical, muscular language makes achieving what you want more possible, more enriched, more satisfying. The actor's job is to pay attention to every hint in the text, to raise questions (but to reject easy answers), so that she can discover what the character's deepest, sometimes masked, desires actually are and to reveal in behavior—even to the author—character-truth.

That which is doable and accomplishable is called an "action." Deep wants that lead to actions can sometimes also lead to the doing of a physical activity, simple or complex. For instance, Hedda Gabler's burning of Lovborg's manuscript is an activity that can be seen as only the last, desperate act of her want, her need, throughout the whole play. The deep want leads to an action, which leads to an activity.

The recognition of a want and doing something about it—an action—is not some esoteric, actor-y idea. In ways big and small, it is part of what we do almost every day of our lives. What do I really want and what am I going to do about getting it? In art and perhaps in life, questions arise about how far am I willing to go to get what I want; how much am I willing to give up; how much am I willing to change? The writer gives you a text as a blueprint. The text leads you, challenges you. It holds secrets. Uncovering them reveals what must be done. Not what could be done, or might be done, or even what should be done in order to accomplish the want. The most rigorous, the most essential, question is: "What must be done?" Whether the immediate answer is the right or final answer is not important in a rehearsal. What matters is that it leads to implementation—that is, doable, accomplishable actions that can be evaluated. The value of immediate implementation is that at the end of the rehearsal, the actor can consider the chosen action and ask, "Did I do it? Did I accomplish what I wanted?"

A suggestion: having chosen a want and an action to accomplish what must be done to get it, it is useful for the actor to continue to ask, "I want such-and-such in order to . . . what?" Saying "in order to" allows you to keep peeling the onion and encourages you not to satisfy yourself with a merely intellectual choice. Keep saying "in order to" and you will get to the kernel. Stop trying to get it right or find a "nice" answer, which only leads to an end of thinking, of creative inquiry. Demand of yourself that you continue to search for a deeper want, a more specific action.

Perhaps not in life, but in art, taking risks is essential. Going too far in rehearsal is essential. Let it be wrong, let it be foolish, let it be shocking. Evaluate it only after you have pursued it as far as possible. Then choose. Dismiss it, repeat it, even choose to keep it. That makes art. The most brilliant, evocative, surprising choice the actor makes about accomplishing the action is what makes art. There should not be any right or wrong. So-called wrong choices, silly, risky choices, often lead to the most artistically satisfying results. These chosen actions, now included in the structure of a performance, come from an actor-artist freed from "trying to get it right," and they best illuminate the playwright's intentions.

THE DESIRED OBSTACLE

On the stage and in life, there is always an obstacle to accomplishing what is wanted. An obstacle is like a rip tide to a swimmer who is trying to reach the shore; it seems so close, but the harder he swims, the more he struggles. With every stroke, there is new effort, whether ultimately futile or heroic. In the work on a play, delineating the obstacle is desirable because it makes it necessary to try different ways to accomplish what is wanted and it creates stronger and more interesting behavior. When strong internal and external desires encounter damnable obstacles, it leads to conflict, on which the theater lives. If the writer doesn't make clear in his work what the obstacles are, it becomes the actor's job to identify, clarify, and intensify them. The courageous, sometimes foolish, sometimes astonishing ways we find to overcome those riptides are what create art.

NOW, IMMEDIACY

Finally, there is immediacy. Actions that attempt to surmount obstacles involve what the actor does. Immediacy informs how the actor does it. A sense of immediacy in performing an action increases the importance and the necessity of accomplishing a want, a desired outcome. Now. Not tomorrow, not later. Right now. Immediacy gives shape and tempo and keeps the character connected to what is essential. In the theater, every writer should make sure that what the character is pursuing has urgency. If the writer has not given the actor a strong enough sense of immediacy, the actor must create it for herself. The famous Russian actor and teacher Maria Ouspenskaya, recognizing her own miserly instincts, said she always played every scene as if there were a taxi downstairs with the meter running. I'm not suggesting that every actor do that, but that was how she heightened her sense of urgency.

Chapter 10
Memory

Brilliant actors, after a long and particularly demanding emotional and physical performance, are often asked by non-actors, "My goodness, how can you remember all those words?" It's like asking a racing-car champion, "How can you remember to do the manual clutch?" Neither for the actor nor the driver does the question have anything to do with being a champion. It is not part of the art, but it is certainly part of each actor's specific craft. Some actors have excellent memories; others have to spend more time memorizing. Some remember best when the text is connected to the physical life on stage; some memorize best with repetition during the rehearsal process. Others can do so only by rote, which requires memorizing mechanically.

I remember rehearsing after I was recently off book (newly memorized) and asking for a forgotten line. I got it from the stage manager, then forgot it a moment later and had to ask for it again (and again!). Not until I stopped, walked over to the stage manager's desk, and looked at the page for a moment did it stick. I learned that I have a visual memory, not an aural one. (Not photographic, either, unfortunately.)

If there is one approach, one imperative, it is this: memorize the content, the expression of an idea, and the need to verbalize the idea that's written. In a long speech, be clear about the content that carries you to the end of what the French call "a tirade." Particularly in a complicated, difficult, hard-to-memorize text, understanding the author's meaning—if not always his way of getting there—will help the actor create a road map that allows the words to be remembered more easily. If suddenly the actor forgets the words but knows the content of what comes next, he'll remember how to say it.

Retention of text is necessary for an actor and is part (though only a small part) of what the actor generously offers to the world of the theater.

I, however, am more interested in other, more mysterious, aspects of our psychological and biological memory systems as they influence the day-to-day work in rehearsal. Applying some memories is easily done. We remember how our great-aunt held her teacup and we use it. We remember how a strange old man sat in a subway and we use it. We also remember the more complicated secrets that we bend and twist to create unconventional and, more important, specific behavior. Every actor discovers, over time, the specific events, traumas perhaps, that bring his instrument to life. As Sanford Meisner told his students at the Neighborhood Playhouse, actors should "place these memories in a golden box, close to the heart, to be used sparingly." Even actors who insist they do not use their history, only their imagination and the text, will find that the play can suddenly trigger a memory that sends them deeper into their own (and the character's) universe.

Human beings have the ability to hold events in memory and call them up at will—in whatever crystal clarity or confusing disorder they arrive. Clearly, memory in all its disguises, and all its false faces, and all its tricks, is an essential tool in the actor's kit.

There are "nostalgic memories." These are quite clear and, even as we relive them now, in the present, evoke in us the same, if somewhat sanitized, anger or joy of the past. Actors make use of these memories and employ them consciously—for instance—to prepare before an entrance or to stimulate the imagination in order to get closer to the character's concerns.

There are memories we've forgotten, what are called "affective memories." Forgotten memories? It seems an oxymoron. Unremembered memories, when discovered by accident or after a search, can be powerful. These are hazily remembered memories, which, when recalled anecdotally, do not bring into the present any of the emotional or physical responsiveness of the past experience. They exist, deeply anchored, and can only be released by some suddenly remembered inconsequential sensory element. They lie quiet and inaccessible. There are instances, however, when such memories arrive uninvited, bringing with them all the original emotion from the past, the hurt or pleasure of the event as it happened. Learning how to access them can be part of the actor's craft.

Affective memories influence the present, working on the physical, intellectual, and emotional life of the actor. They are full, perhaps, of provocative and challenging emotional elements—either magnificently positive or painfully negative—and they can lead to surprising behavior. Because buried memories can be so potent, and strongly affective, the exercise needed to discover and then use them requires artistic insight, personal discretion, and craft. Affective memory as a

87

craft tool for actors was first explored by Stanislavski. Since then, its efficacy, its value, and even its dangers have been hotly argued. Two of the greatest acting teachers, Stella Adler and Lee Strasberg, never reconciled on this issue.

My own, not very original, response to this discussion is that the use of the affective memory exercise, even its value as a tool, should depend totally on, first, the particular actor, then the specific experience to be excavated, and finally, of course, the play-problem needing to be solved. The affective memory exercise, once its use is learned and practiced, is for heavy lifting. If there are other tools, more simple problem-solvers, they should be explored first.

LITERATURE'S MOST FAMOUS COOKIE

Perhaps the most famous example of an affective memory in literature is found in Marcel Proust's description of a cookie and a cup of tea, which appears at the end of the first chapter of *Swann's Way*. Proust did not discover affective memory; psychologists already knew about it. For the actor, in addition to the miracle of memory tied to a specific object, what is important about Proust and the tea and the little sea-shell cookie (the famous madeleine) is that Proust discovered that the more he tried to re-experience the sudden upsurge of acute emotion (in order to discover its origin), the less emotion he felt. Only when he grew tired of trying and just drank the tea and ate the madeleine did the feeling return, and with it the memory of his morning with his aunt and the tea and cookies he had shared with her. If you the actor want the fullness of an experience again, do not pursue a result. Just drink the tea and eat the madeleine. Acting is doing.

MAMMALIAN MEMORY

Memory remains mysterious—how we use it, how we lose it, and how we reclaim it. In 2013, the *New York Times* reported that a Nobel Laureate, Dr. Sasumu Tonegawa, and his associates had discovered a part of the mammalian brain (or at least the mouse and human brain) that can create completely false memories—memories the brain accepts as truth.[2] Fabricating lies like truth. Sound familiar? Of course. It is exactly what we actors do. The playwright suggests a made-up story, a fabrication. Then we actors with our talent, craft, and willing brain begin to believe it. Our behavior changes, our relationships are rearranged, and for a while the lie seems absolutely like the truth. Dr. Tonegawa asked, "Why is our brain made in such a way that we form false memories? No one knows."

---

2. James Gorman, "Science traces memories that never happened," *New York Times* (July 26, 2013).

Chapter 11
Listening to the Body

In 1941, the Neighborhood Playhouse School of the Theatre was a primary training ground for actors. Irene Lewisohn and Rita Morganthau were the two magnificent women, the financial as well as spiritual organizers, who put their money where their hearts were. They were wise enough to make their school the domain of a great acting teacher, Sanford Meisner. He and his class at the Playhouse, as well as his professional classes, represented the best of actor training for the next forty years.

But we men and women, aspiring and hopeful young actors, when we arrived at 9:00 a.m. at the Playhouse on 46th Street, we belonged to and were at the mercy of another giant, Martha Graham. Unbelievably, Martha Graham. Playing rehearsal pianist with her was Louis Horst, Martha's physical and artistic muse. Martha (as she insisted on being called), in addition to being a pioneer of modern dance, was one of the most important and influential innovators in the history of American performance. Sandy and the school felt that an actor's expressive, responsive body needed as much development as his internal instrument.

All of Martha Graham's work concerned storytelling—stories about the Greeks, stories about Emily Dickinson. And all the stories were told only with the body. They were complete, emotionally involving, and revelatory. That is the world of the dance, but from it we can learn how important and generous the body can be when there's something we want to accomplish. The theater, as well as dance, wants the body to amplify psychological and emotional truth.

Our bodies always want to come to our aid when we want to make something clear, to get something accomplished. Famously, when asked to describe a spiral staircase, everyone's hand, whatever their language, makes a circle in the air. Ask someone to describe a Van Dyke beard, and his hand will tell you. The body seeks to help us accomplish what must be done; it is anxious to be part of the process. Whatever else the actor develops in himself as he trains, he must recognize that a responsive body is part of the process.

Too often, actors are intellectually and emotionally involved but do not encourage their body to take part. These actors are, in theatrical shorthand, "talking heads." Unfortunately (at least for actors), we have been taught from childhood to suppress, to deny, sometimes to not even notice what the body is telling us. Afraid of looking foolish or behaving inappropriately, we tend to reject useful body behavior that can influence character-behavior and reveal, unconventionally, internal wants. Good acting is often a result of the body's nonintellectualized, idiosyncratic, physical responses to a given situation.

THE BODY-BRAIN

When the actor is most concentrated, working most truthfully (enriched by his understanding of the psychology of the character and by his own choices), the body is most apt to respond on its own,

91

to encourage, to insist, and to push the actor to risk. If we're truthful and we're present, our body speaks, sometimes amplifying, and sometimes in opposition to, what is written. These physical responses can reveal interesting information about what is happening to the character.

There is another dimension to body response. Humans have a mysterious way of getting information that is absolute and which arrives with a certainty that cannot be denied and which usually demands action. It does not come from what we understand as the conscious brain. "I don't know what it was, but I just felt uncomfortable," or "I don't have a reason, but I don't trust him," or "Something told me . . ." or "I have a gut feeling." And the best: "I just felt happy and I don't know why." There are many instances in which our responses, our sensibility, arrive powerfully from somewhere within us other than our thinking-brain. We might even insist that we have a "sixth sense" about somebody or something. It is not our conscious evaluating process that creates the response. Perhaps the best example is falling in love at first sight—when the body, not the mind, leads the way.

Children are marvelously attuned to unreasoned body responses. They rely on and respond to sudden physical feelings—about food, about people, about noise, about music. Ask a child, "Why don't you like him, dear? He's your uncle," and you will not get a logical response. I have been rewarded while reading the newspaper by a five-year-old son, who, for no discernible reason, rushed over and kissed me. There were things that that child's body needed to express, and he had no filter that prevented him from behaving.

What is important for the actor is that he bring to his work a body with all the doors unlatched and all the windows open so that he can catch every wisp of what comes from the body-brain as well as what comes from the thinking-brain.

When actors try to explain their spontaneous behavior, the tendency is to sanitize, to make their responses less animal, less raw. By sanitizing, they remove from the given situation the most basic, personally connected, and—more important—behavior-producing action.

In a rehearsal, the body, like a child's body, should be allowed to lead the actor beyond what has been decided ahead of time. Rather than trying to articulate the reasons for our surprising reactions, it is better to explore the body for the response: lean farther in, lean back, shrink farther away, or confront aggressively. Get up and dance because you are given good news—the body will be grateful. If the body response is positive, be willing in the rehearsal to kiss your partner for no discernible script reason, or just hug him. Such exploration, of course, should not include uncivil behavior toward the other actor. Remember that your partner has physical responses that you might not like!

Sometimes, I ask actors to choreograph their monologues, using the text as an internal road map to physicalize the monologue silently without being illustrative. Or I tell them simply to dance spontaneously as they experience the text. Movement of this kind helps find new meanings, clarity in the text, and releases interesting and useful behavior that was stifled when only the text was used. Singing the text also releases experiences that the actor may not be allowing the body to pursue. Singing without vocal strain vibrates the emotional strings, freeing the actor to behave in unexpected emotional as well as physical ways. This fullest kind of exploration in rehearsal gives the actor (and the director) a larger, more varied palette from which to choose the most artistically valuable responses, while also giving the work of the actor more life, more zip, more taste.

Of course, you will worry about how the world will respond if you follow what is, in that moment of physical exploration, fully organic but which may seem illogical to others. Don't worry. Don't censor. To give the author, the director, and finally the audience the best of you means to rehearse, to dare to investigate, if only for yourself, the immediate, truthful, spontaneous moment. Six out of ten explorations will be worthless. But the eighth! That extraordinary moment never would have revealed itself without a welcoming artist. (The seventh, ninth, and tenth were only acceptable.)

Yes, but . . . "What if I feel no desire to move?" Don't wait until you "feel like" moving. You're waiting to move because you want to be truthful emotionally. But actor-truth is "I am where I am." The stage direction may say that your character is so angry, he slaps his partner. It may be that you're not ready to slap. But acting is not passive. Even if you're not ready, stand up. Even if you're not ready, walk over. Even if you're not ready, lift your hand and slap him. Believe me, by then you will be ready. When you don't try to "feel like" it, you will be surprised at how much more readily the inner demands of the situation rise to the surface.

The film director, in a close-up, tells you, "Don't move around so much." It's a bad suggestion. It's counterproductive because what the director really wants is for you to go deeper, more internal. Casual movement dissipates the energy and the through line of what your character is saying. Stillness, the quiet breath, is powerful and very active. In stillness, all the energy and all the compulsions turn internal, deeper, more urgent, and they urgently affect the other.

Pay attention to the unconscious messages the body is trying to encourage. Make sure the body understands that you're available, that you want its help. Allowing your body to help you clarify the best possible ways of accomplishing what must be done will finally bring you to own, to embody, what you are creating.

Yet nothing in this discussion should in any way neglect or deny the importance of the actor's intellectual interest, curiosity, the actor's imagining of the writer's "idée fixe" that creates the work at hand. It is only from this and its stirring of the actor's creative juices that one can expect the body to lead. A liberated body amplifies and illuminates the intellect. Craft, finally, is how to put together, in the rehearsal, the spoken word, the exciting ideas embedded in the text, the challenges from the other actors, and the actor's personal responses, both conscious and unconscious.

III.

In Performance

Chapter 12
Preparation: Internal and External

I am excluding the larger implications of the word "preparation," that is, what happens after the phone call saying the actor has the job, the big part, the game changer: rearranging family life, calling the dialect coach, or even a night on the street if you are playing a homeless person. Preparation here is discussed as a tool as you prepare a performance—and during it. It's a battery charge that enables the actor-artist to bring his presence, his here and now, into the imaginary world of the writer.

FIRST, GETTING TO NEUTRAL

Whether preparing oneself to transform into another human being in a series of short takes in a film or for a long night of storytelling in the theater, it is useful to cleanse oneself of the real-world, problem-solving daily routines before starting a specific preparation. Create an inner space that is quiet, muscularly relaxed, concentrated, and unconnected to yesterday or today. Stay away from the future. Now, only the easy breath. Neutral.

Getting to neutral is a craft decision that allows the actor to give himself to the writer, uninhibited and unobstructed, in the most creative way. Beginning in neutral encourages the fullest attention to the other actors and creates an empty interior space to be filled by the circumstances of the play.

Neutral comes first, even when the very hurly-burly of the immediate present is exactly what the actor wants in order to ready herself. So make no rules. What is always wanted is a specific choice, arrived at by trial and error. Do not concern yourself with "Is this neutral? Am I there?" There is no "there." What is most important is the effort you make to move to neutral. You've done what you can, and whatever now remains—whatever concerns and real-life upsets that are still present—will be part of what you bring to the imaginary world. Do not spend any effort denying yourself. It is only the effort to begin at that empty place that matters.

How now does the actor in neutral move into the story? The practiced actor learns, through years of work, what she will do upon arrival at the workplace. Neutral, perhaps, and then beyond. The theater makes its own special demands. First, ignore the "half hour" call. That's for the stage manager to know he has a full company. Arrive early. Structure your time once you get to the workplace. I knew a very good actor who did a five-minute headstand before every play. I envied his ability and respected his rigor. Others choose quiet meditation. Still others listen to music or do yoga.

Entering the imaginary world—every night, every take—wants a start, a kick-off; every actor needs to explore, to test, to make choices. Depending on the actor, on the playwright, and on the particular situation and relationships of the play, the choices for the actor as she prepares to move into the bright light of the imaginary world are limitless. Plan, then, what will be the most creative and concentrated tasks to bring you closer to this new world. These preparations, whether energizing or quieting, should concentrate, stimulate, and provoke the necessity of your entrance onto the stage.

INTERNAL AND EXTERNAL PREPARATION

An internal preparation means that the actor, at the moments before his entrance, must find, deeply anchored within himself, an understanding of the character's needs. It is this inner connection that makes his entrance necessary. Sometimes, and for some actors, just the story of the play, the previous events, are enough to create a strong and truthful inner life. At other times, accessing the actor's personal history can move him directly into the character's present and make the character's emotional response directly available for the actor, lifting it above the heart and into the mouth. Over time, the actor discovers just where the internal buttons are—what I call the ignition switches—so that they can be accessed when needed. It is that deeper, internal exploration that will lead to the most evocative result.

External preparation concerns the physical state of the character (and the actor!). Every role needs a heightened and even nervous energy; it needs to have oxygen sent to the brain. Help the diaphragm fill itself by stretching the muscles around the rib cage. Many parts need an energizing exercise, some more, some less—but every scene requires strengthening the flow of blood into the muscles and into the brain. No matter the scene, acting demands the most vibrant, responsive body. Depending on the space and the costume, do push-ups or knee-bends, maybe shadow-boxing. You will most likely be nervous. Nervousness is useful. Nerves, the elevated heartbeat, even shortness of breath, are part of the body's aliveness. Don't try to control it, deny it, or get rid of it. Allow the nervousness. Turn your heightened nervousness into an energized entrance. A classical text, no matter the internal work, will certainly want vocal and body preparation. Play Tybalt in *Romeo and Juliet* and you'd better warm up, physically, for the duel. Play Mercutio and, for that lover of language, you'll need a serious vocal warm-up for his ode to Queen Mab. For classical plays an actor will want both physical and vocal warm-ups.

Of course, every entrance in every play and in every scene requires its own impulse. Almost always, it can be helpful to begin the activity that's happening before your entrance and to continue it as you come on. Giving yourself to those activities can affect internal as well as external behavior. Often, however, logical physical behavior is not enough. What is most important is concentration on the character's internal concerns, as well as what she wants now. That means ignoring what the actor, having read and rehearsed the play, knows is about to happen. Entering, the actor is concerned only with the need that brings the character to the moment of coming on stage.

You will say, "But suppose the character kills himself at the end of the scene. Shouldn't that affect the way I enter?" The answer is: probably not. In most cases, it's best, theatrically, to play one choice at a time completely before the next possibility arises. Take, as an example, Treplev in Chekhov's *The Seagull*. He has trouble working creatively; he longs for Nina who has been away for a number of years. She returns, but even as Treplev tries to make her stay, she leaves again. Treplev then commits suicide. As the actor lives through the scene, the most important thing is how desperately Treplev needs Nina to stay with him and how certain he is that he can convince her to stay. The stronger the actor's belief that he can win, the harder it will be for Nina to leave. Treplev must fight to keep her with him until he is exhausted and forced to confront the realization that the fight is over. It is only when Nina leaves that we see develop in front of us Treplev's impossibility of living without her. The actor should have no conscious thought of suicide during the scene.

Every actor constructs her own roadmap, which requires researching and discovering within herself the kind of preparation, the "ignition," she will need. Uta Hagen, in Act I, Scene 3 of *The Country Girl*, always stood in the wings, watching the scene before her entrance, focused on the characters on stage and what they were saying about her character, while chewing an enormous wad of pink bubble gum. Just before she entered, she would pull the wad out of her mouth, press it onto the wall, and on she'd go. That was her preparation for the scene. Years later, I asked her about the bubble gum. She told me that the hard chewing was an energizing exercise and that listening to her husband tell lies about her lit her fuse.

Finally, in the moment of "the entrance," what matters most, more than energizing, or the necessary emotional involvement, is the actor's ability to bring to it a muscularly relaxed, fully concentrated, and therefore accessible instrument. Trust that all the thought, the work leading up to this moment, will be there to support you. And breathe. The natural instinct as one jumps into the pool is to take a deep breath and hold it as you go in. Reject it! Enter on the exhale. Inhale as you begin to change the character's world.

FILM PREPARATION

The only absolute for a film actor's preparation is the impossibility of discussing a film actor's preparation. In the theater, when the players arrive at the workplace, it is always the same. The time sequences are the same. Every night the same. How the rest of the night reveals itself is always wonderfully variable, but we can still count on what used to be called the "call boy" letting the actors know, "Fifteen minutes, please . . . five minutes, folks . . ." and always from the actors a big "Thank you!" and finally, "Places!" and the heart starts beating faster. Then always the command "Curtain!" (even when there isn't one).

In film, the one thing to count on is that you will get ready—makeup, clothes, hair—and then you will wait. And wait. And wait. Wait on location today, wait tomorrow in a studio. Plan for long waiting times. Bring a particular book that will help you stop thinking about yourself or about how you will play the scene. Stay grounded. What lies ahead is, at best, a series of improvisations.

Being clear about what the character was doing directly before the entrance, before the word "action," is basic and fruitful, just as it is in the theater. Some work will want you to stay quiet. Or you will decide that it is useful to chat with colleagues before "We need you." Hope that it won't be "Hurry, we need you now." If you have some warning, check the breath, make sure you are allowing the breath to go deep, that it is relaxed and regular. Use the trip from the trailer to the set as a relaxing exercise. Then, just for yourself so that no one will know, it might be useful to live physically and emotionally—secretly—as the character, even talk as the character while talking to a stagehand, a costumer, even as you walk to your mark. But stay away from "rehearsing," going over how you will do what you will do. Remember: it's an improvisation.

While filming, even when you're given a daily schedule, it is almost impossible for the production to stick to it. The place and the pace of filming can change day to day. And for any one take, you cannot prepare for the whole story (even if you are lucky enough to be part of it). Your character will win the baseball World Series on the first day of shooting, and then the rest of his days on the set will be spent in the minor leagues.

But there is a very real gift in these difficulties. Filming demands and encourages spontaneity. In the theater, the actor works to make it happen "for the first time." In filming it often is the first time; no rehearsal is possible. Film wants a sense of inner improvising. Even the exact repeat is an interesting challenge. Challenge and artistic problem-solving is where the performer thrives. Remember that what made you commit yourself to a life in acting is the risk, the danger, of being totally alive in each moment as you work—unsure, worried . . . but alive!

PREPARATION FOR DIFFERENT KINDS OF ACTORS

There is much talk, even argument, about whether a specific actor works internally or externally, both in preparation and in the living-through of the performance. Such pinpointing is foolish and useless. All good actors do both. But I believe that no matter where the actor begins, internally or externally, when he is able to connect his private self unflinchingly to the inner truth that the play demands, and when that internal truth is deeply anchored, the more it is revealed by the external behavior. Over years, an actor develops the best beginning place. Some actors begin instinctively by developing a strong physical outline, while others need to work internally before there is any physical change. For a good actor, the starting gate will often depend on the specific role or the culture of the play and even the culture of the playwright.

Ruth White, a brilliant actor, and I were in John Carradine's production of *Tobacco Road*, a play about the poorest of the displaced farm people during the Great Depression. Ruth arrived at the first rehearsal in the most worn-out, torn-apart, toes-showing shoes. "What's up with the shoes?" I asked. Ruth, a very inner-directed actor ("Method," we would say today) said—and I'm quoting exactly here—"I always start with the feet, darling." The next day, as a joke, I came into rehearsal barefoot. I don't know whether it was funny, but I was surprised to find it useful. I went shoeless for the rest of the rehearsals. Fifteen years later, Ruthie was Samuel Beckett's first-ever Winnie in *Happy Days*, playing a character buried in sand for the whole play. I've always wondered what was on her feet.

THE MASK, THE UNMASKED, AND THE MASK THAT REVEALS

Some fine actors have found that no matter how close they are to the character that's written, they need some small, perhaps invisible, physical change—a different hairstyle, a mustache, reshaped eyebrows, a nose change, an always-too-tight shirt collar or blouse. These changes are a kind of mask, behind which the actor is more able to live and reveal the deepest personal truth. Of course, these actors also delight in becoming, character to character, physically unrecognizable. It has been said that, in the best clown work, the red nose is the smallest mask, allowing the inner fool to become public. This breed of actor wants to look in the mirror and not recognize himself. Think of Laurence Olivier or Meryl Streep. (Streep is a great mimic. Her ability to become Margaret Thatcher or Julia Child has in it her extraordinary mimetic instincts as well as her stunning acting talents.)

Sometimes the external change is so small only the actor knows it has been added. Noël Coward, acting in one of his own plays, wore cotton underwear in the first act, linen in the second act, and silk in the third. He was never undressed in the play; he did it for himself. Women, too, will choose specific underclothes early in the rehearsal process. No one need see the change.

There are other fine actors who work most truthfully when there is nothing added, nothing standing between them and the audience. They always—necessarily—bring different selves, but they are always completely recognizable. Think of Marlon Brando or Kevin Spacey. Brando always located the depth of the soul of the character through his own visible sensibility. Whether as Marc Antony or Stanley Kowalski, Brando was totally visible, yet strikingly metamorphosed, bringing insight and believability to the particular character.

There have always been serious, important actors who demand of themselves that they connect their own internal world to that of the character before making the necessary external choices. And there have always been excellent actors whose talent lies primarily in their ability to create the extraordinary physical look, sound, and behavior of a character in both comedies and serious plays. Actor-artists always bring, with the help of the writer, a sudden, sharp, recognizable humanity, a truthful window on who we are.

Chapter 13
In Performance

Opening night. You stand in the wings, heart beating rapidly. The stage manager says, "Places!" You hear your cue. That moment, before your first entrance into the world of the play, no matter how deeply rehearsed you are, that moment, in every performance, is the most transformative moment in the life of the actor.

An actor who has never experienced a live audience cannot fully know that moment. A director calling "Action!" on a film set is close—but it is not the same. Experiencing a live audience, with all its joys and terrors, is an essential part of the actor's initial desire to live in imaginary circumstances—and all of that joy and terror is in that first offstage moment. It has in it both the best and sometimes the most frightening elements of why we do what we do. The actor about to enter is always at the edge of the precipice, always on the high diving board for the first time. Before that moment, everything is preparation. Making an entrance opens the door to the potential for art.

The fullest experience of acting cannot exist without an audience.

Rehearsal is rehearsal. Even the final dress rehearsal is still a rehearsal, and though it is collaborative and full of its own joys and satisfactions, it is not yet art. All the hope, all the discoveries, and even the despair of the rehearsals must now be shared with an audience.

The pain and the pleasure of that moment before the curtain goes up can keep some actors in the theater or drive other very good actors away. What we call "stage fright," that unreasoned primal fear, which is intellectually ridiculous but psychologically wounding, brings with it sudden bladder needs, dry mouth, elevated heartbeat, and the aptly named "flop sweat." But more often, and more important, there can be in that "before the entrance" moment challenge, edgy excitement, anticipation, the tingle of the adrenaline rush, and visceral aliveness. For the actor this is the high point and it keeps some of us in the theater despite all the obvious obstacles to such a life. Everything the actor does has led to this existential moment of creating a life in theater.

To paraphrase Vladimir Nemirovich-Danchenko, the brilliant codirector of the Moscow Art Theatre: build a beautiful building, fill it with an orchestra, an excellent producer and director, magnificent sets—still there will be no theater. There will only be a well-kept building. But when three actors come to an open space, spread a small rug on the ground, and begin to perform—there is theater.

For there to be theater, there must be the actor. I would add that there must be the audience. Nothing else is essential. The commedia dell'arte, particularly in the sixteenth and seventeenth centuries, had no writer. It was the primary theatrical experience for most of the Western world. It was comic, and the comedy was vulgar, improvised, based on character, and driven by the actor. It had repeated behavior, situations, jokes—"lazzi," they were called—but no writer. It was theater of the streets, and however wise about the human condition, it wanted nothing but to make you laugh—at the "other" and at yourself. But it isn't enough.

It was never enough. Actors need writers—especially great writers. Perhaps the greatest gift of commedia is that from it came Molière, who helped us see past the laugh and under it. Actors need writers, especially the great writers. Almost two millennia before commedia, Greco-Roman writers gave their audiences similar slapstick comedy. Those audiences were also given Oedipus, Medea, and Electra. For theater to be challenging, inspiring, even revelatory, to reach the heart, the theater and the actor must have the artist-writer who is committed to challenging us with new insights that gloriously illuminate the human condition. The artist-writer challenges the actor to bring the writer's view of humankind to audience. It is the writer whose work continues on down through the ages.

Sarah Siddons, Edmund Kean, and Eleonora Duse turned mediocre melodramas into heart-pounding theater, but they needed the Shakespeares and the Ibsens in order to realize their full potential as actors. How sad that we only get those magnificent performances secondhand, through the writing of critics. Who would not give the world to have seen Burbage in Shakespeare's *Hamlet*? As a young man in the 1920s, Lee Strasberg saw Duse, and it changed his life. Literally. Elia Kazan, hearing Lee talk about that experience, twice set up midnight meetings (after all of Broadway's curtains had come down) for actors to come to his rehearsal studio to listen to Strasberg describe Duse's acting. And Strasberg, astonishingly, stopped in the middle, weeping. I watched as Kazan put his arm around Lee, comforting him until he regained his composure.

However heart-pounding the theatrical experience on any given night, it is lost forever. This is the essential despair of live theater. [3]

THE THEATRICAL TRIANGLE

Theater is commonly understood as a collaboration-in-performance of writer-actor-audience. The intuitive view of this collaboration is that the writer is primary. Superficially, this would seem true. But in the creation of a meaningful theatrical experience, on the night of the performance, the collaboration must be an equilateral triangle—three equal sides. I am saying that the audience, the writer, and the actor are of equal importance, each depending on the other to create theater.

It begins, of course, with the writer. But what the playwright creates, the play on the page, is literature. However beautiful and magnificent the dramatist's language, however startling the situations and compelling the characters as written, it is not yet theater. The playwright takes his work and hands the text to the actor: "Here," he says with some trepidation, "with your help, we can make it theater." Sometimes this gift (because the text is a gift) is misunderstood and misused by actors. Trashed and caricatured, it becomes theater, but bad theater. But sometimes—I might even say most times—the text inspires the actors to bring the playwright's world to vivid, impassioned life, creating from it off-the-page, three-dimensional human beings never before seen. Even the writer will feel exhilaration.

Still, it is not yet theater. It has to be taken before an audience. And what would be best: a large audience. Actors like a full house. They ask, "How's the house?" They thrive on the energy of a packed

---

3. The New York Public Library for the Performing Arts, situated in Lincoln Center, films at least every play that opens on Broadway and gives us an idea of what was.

crowd. The audience, too, likes to sit amidst the excitement of a full house, the excited buzz before the curtain rises. The lights dim, the house gets quiet, and there is that breath-holding pause of anticipation. And then, when the stage manager says, "Curtain," the miracle of theater begins.

What does the actor bring to this extraordinary event?

CRAFT, EXPERIENCE, AND ART

Art for the actor is not some overblown, meaningless generalization. It has in it the visceral pleasure of sharing the deepest part of oneself: the excitement and the doubts of aiming where failure is real and where quiet, enriched accomplishment lies waiting.

The actor-artist's contribution, his part of the theatrical triangle, is to inhabit and experience the character the playwright has created and to do so in every word, every relationship, every situation. This requires at the very beginning many close readings of the text. It also means reading the playwright's other plays to, as Shakespeare put it in another context, "pluck out the heart of his mystery, sound him from his lowest note to the top of his compass." Included in this mystery is how the writer developed, how he arrived at this particular work. Read Tennessee Williams's early one-acters if you want to do *A Streetcar Named Desire*. Read Harold Pinter's early short plays to understand *The Homecoming*. Read Sam Shepard of the sixties to play his work of the eighties.

The ability of the actor to express the writer's language with intellectual clarity is not enough. It is not enough to speak the text intelligently and with feeling, not enough even to speak it with understanding, subtlety, color, light, and shadow. Being "on the words" is not enough. Think of an iceberg and the chunk of ice visible above the water. It is beautiful, even magnificent, startling in its light and shadows. But what is astonishing, dangerous, and thrilling is what is below the water—a hundred times larger than your wildest imagination can conceive. I suggest the piece of iceberg above the surface is the text, which of course cannot exist without that mountain below. Some playwrights demand, "Say my words distinctly, clearly, and I'll have what I want." But in my experience with playwrights, the best of them are grateful and thrilled when the actor, with her deep involvement, reveals something in the text the writer didn't quite know was there or illuminates what he hoped was there.

To give Shakespeare's prose and poetry its full richness and resonance is rewarding and unfortunately rare. But it is not enough, not even for Shakespeare, about whom it is often said, "Everything is in the text; there is no subtext." That is not so. It cannot be so. No human being exists without the possibility of a subtext that is ongoing, motivating, quick to the surface, or even carefully hidden. We all can lie in the words or keep the truth unspoken. There are, of course, times in the performing of any great playwright's works when living mainly through the text is primary, when it is essential to continue driving forward with language. It is only then that a sudden stop, a realization, can have some meaningful result.

Therefore, and most important, the actor must work to discover the human experience the playwright is excavating. It is useful for the actor to create his own backstory, to improvise scenes and events not included in the time span of the play. This deep immersion into the heart (and maybe the soul) of a good writer's work must begin and then continue in rehearsal as the actor begins to look within himself to find connections to the character that are revealing and emotionally surprising and which will influence much of the character's behavior.

There will be times when the actor's specific detailed memories, physical and emotional, can influence the play's action and relationships, not with superficial tears but in the most idiosyncratic, character-truthful, and shattering ways. At other times, the actor's history is only the beginning, the ignition switch of the actor's internal motor. The actor must always be willing to go further, to open wide the door of his imagination and allow the given circumstances of the play and the behavior of the other actors to surprise, unsettle, and create the unexpected, the unlooked for. The mysterious ways in which actors blend their imaginations, fantasies, and personal histories into the fabric of the play are difficult to quantify. They are often not fully understood, even by the artist.

There are many actors who have no desire to use personal history, who want only to use their imagination and the story of the play. I think that's fine. When those two create an unconventional and satisfying truth, that is just as one would like it. But what happens when the actor's intuition lies quiet? Then tools and techniques are required: craft. Then the conscious use of personal history, the ability to use it artistically, is often what pulls the actor most deeply into the play.

Interestingly, there are times when the actor, rejecting personal history, wanting only the story of the play and the actor's imagination to lead her, is suddenly more deeply affected than she expected to be. Her intuitive response shocks and surprises her. Most likely it is because her unconscious has offered a deeply buried personal connection. If that is true, then when the actor's intuition is quiet, when the truth of the play is not forthcoming, when only the intellect is alive, why not learn, through craft, to access personal history? After years of work, an actor develops a personal technique that conflates the detailed circumstances of the play, the immediate present that surrounds her, and elements of her past that can inform the play's present.

There are actors who are so self-involved, so concerned only with their own experience (as important as that may be), that they limit what the playwright wants of them and act the text with only self-absorbed emotionalism. This is a violation of what Stanislavski understood and the system he developed. It is a caricature of what was taught by the best acting teachers of the twentieth century—some of whom are the children, grandchildren, and great-grandchildren of Konstantin and who too often are held responsible for bad actors acting badly.

THE ACTOR AND THE AUDIENCE

The most generous, the most essential thing the actor can offer the audience is the deepest, most experienced, most craft-illuminated self. A self that is character delineated but unadorned, unmuddied by ego pressures, and with what the actor understands as character-truth. By offering that "self," a particular truth can reach the audience so directly and so powerfully that its breathing is altered, casual movements cease, and its concentration deepens significantly. Actors know when they are having that kind of effect on the audience, that moment in a play when they're "in the zone," when the actor, totally engrossed in the life of the play, can suddenly in that audience silence sense the change. That moment is addictive. And it is elusive.

As a young actor, my first taste of becoming aware that every audience member was breathing with me, was present with me, waiting for the next moment, was in the summer of 1942. Five friends and I went to Pearl Lake Lodge in the Catskill Mountains—the Borscht Belt—as entertainers. Every night we did something different—concert, vaudeville, games, and theater! For one night only, we performed an abbreviated version of a Clifford Odets play about Nazi Germany before the war, *Till the Day I Die*. It was very agitprop, written the same year as his best-known agitprop play, *Waiting for Lefty*. My close friend and colleague, Dolph Green, played a resistance fighter and I played a Nazi major who had to elicit a confession from him. In this scene, instead of using torture and the threat of the concentration camp, my character, who was never committed to Nazism, decides to let him escape. In that moment, knowing that by my action I am now doomed, I decide to shoot myself. After Dolph exited, I remember sitting quietly on the stage for a moment, thinking about what to do, a moment I had not taken in our quick rehearsals. Suddenly I felt the stillness of the audience, felt them holding their breath even as I was breathing quietly and deeply. Though totally connected to the dilemma of the Nazi major, I became aware that the audience and I were experiencing this together. Now I opened a drawer and took out a gun. I lifted the gun to my head. Blackout.

The audience and the actor were together in an event written by the playwright, the three of us equally creating this moment. I had never experienced such awareness. It was my first taste of both communing with an audience and in the same instant living in the world of the play. Unhurried, it was an enlightened moment for me.

I know now that this moment happened because during the pause (the pause I had not taken in rehearsal), it occurred to me to remove my swastika armband, which, unfortunately, had been pinned to my shirt, presenting me with a problem I now had to solve. My concentration, my unhurried attention to unfastening the pin, removing the armband, opening the drawer, taking out a gun—my focus on each part of that action—is what created my communion with the audience. Actor concentration creates audience concentration. My attention to my actions deepened the audience's involvement in what they were experiencing. I had resisted "acting," resisted making "drama." Only the pause, the stillness, unmoving, simply actor-character/character-actor thinking of what to do next, was key.

THE PAUSE

In the performing arts, there are many words for the pause: caesura, fermata, the shock moment, rest, silence. And it does not exist only in art.

In baseball—bottom of the ninth, one run behind, best pitcher facing best hitter at the plate, forty-five thousand people caught in the moment. Notice the pitcher as he leans forward, deeply concentrated on the fingers of the catcher some sixty feet away, suggesting a pitch. This deeply concentrated, stop-action pause continues if the pitcher's head moves, ever so slightly left and right, negatively, while the catcher suggests a different pitch. Again, the fingers sign. The pitcher agrees. And then the pause is over and the mechanics of throwing a ball ninety-five miles an hour resumes.

In the theater, perhaps even more than in life, the pause can be as serious, as meaningful, as the most well-crafted sentence. It is never without content, important or not, to the hearer (in this case, to an audience). There are many different kinds of pauses: stop-action, stop-verbal, inadvertent, illuminating, brilliantly chosen, or pointless and ill advised.

In performance, the general pause, the unchosen, casual "thinking" pause sprinkled throughout the work makes the artful pause meaningless. I disagree with those who tell the actor not to speak until she believes what she is about to say. Even in rehearsal it destroys immediacy, impedes discovering tempo and logic, and is essentially untruthful and egocentric. At best, such an idea is a teaching tool for an actor unable (or unwilling) to think beneath the words. The technical demand to "pick up your cue" is a creative idea. Go forward with the text (but don't indicate the emotional content, don't lie). In life we want to find a response—we're anxious to respond. We have wants and needs that must be fulfilled, in most cases with words (together with actions). Even when we're not sure what to say or how to say it, we tend to begin speaking and to think as we speak. It's good advice for the actor.

The effort should always be to want to answer, even if the actor is displeased with what's written, or even if he chooses not to speak the whole line. But do begin the line; always begin it on cue. The need to speak propels the actor verbally forward, even when the character or the actor isn't completely committed to what's being said. Go on with the text. Whether you believe the line or not, go forward with what is truthful for you in that moment. In life, we often find ourselves speaking and, not happy with what we're saying, we'll think or say, "I don't know why I said that; it's not what I mean." So it is for the character, even if it can't be verbalized.

Sometimes a character may be confronted with an extraordinary, unexpected event. The search to respond satisfactorily can result in a very alive, verbal halt. In that case, it's not because the character wants to pause. Quite the opposite. It's because she is overwhelmed, looking desperately for a way to answer, to speak. It is not necessary that she must want to say exactly what the author finally has her say. Sometimes, something is done or said which so surprises, disturbs, angers, or even pleases, that no matter what's written, the actor's response cannot, for a moment, be verbal ("I'm at a loss for words!"). There is a pause, but the desire is urgently, even desperately, to answer. It may take the form of a physical act, an exit, a slap, a hug, a laugh. But, finally, the written line must be said.

Great writers weave moments of silence in between their words. Harold Pinter understood the loudness of a silent pause; he understood the fermata. I am told he would concern himself with the difference between a two-beat pause and a three-beat pause. He knew the pause contains as much music, as much content, as a trumpet blast. Pinter does not tell the actor what to think, only that the character's universe stops for a moment. In *Waiting for Godot*, Samuel Beckett makes a distinction between a "pause," a "short pause," a "long pause," and a "silence."

Philip Seymour Hoffman, at the very beginning of his performance as Willy Loman in *Death of a Salesman* in 2012, entered with his suitcase, stopped center stage, put down the suitcase, and stood for a long moment, breathing as the world turned. A chosen silence. A pause. He was home. His pause revealed character, situation, and Willy's relationship to his world. The actor, willing to trust himself, had chosen to simply be present. In that pause, he encouraged the audience to begin to question, to become involved—"What's he thinking? What happens now?"

In every positive example of what I am calling a pause, it must move the event forward, even more deeply than it could with language.

CHEKHOV, *THE CHERRY ORCHARD*, AND THE PAUSE

When the Moscow Art Theatre came to the United States in the 1950s, it brought a repertoire of plays, including their production of *The Cherry Orchard*, which I went to see with enormous excitement. Finally I was going to see what I had read, what I had studied. It begins with a few lines of dialogue that announce the imminent arrival of the main characters, Lyubov Ranevskaya, her brother, and her daughter. The servants, Dunyasha and Lopakhin, rush off to meet them. In the Moscow Art Theatre production, there were the expected offstage sounds of the arrival, and then . . . silence. I sat there, expecting that in a moment the characters would rush in and the play would move forward. But there was just silence. Nothing. A pause. Then suddenly, an explosion of laughter. Obviously, someone in the offstage greeting had told a joke. Then silence again. Pause. I, who had been on the edge of my chair, relaxed. I began now to imagine the world that was going on offstage. There were calls, loud talk, silences. I sat back, happy to be led by my own memories of homecomings fully into Chekhov's world.

At the end of the play, there are three extraordinary pauses, silences, when the verbal life, the written dialogue, is over but where life needs to continue beyond language. The beloved home of the main characters, the place of their well-remembered childhoods and the orchard in which they played, has been sold. The house is to be destroyed; the cherry trees will be cut down. The house is empty; all are waiting in the carriage. Only Lyubov and her brother Gayev, who grew up here, remain in the nursery. They walk to the door, and looking back, Lyubov says her last line: "One last look at these walls . . . mother loved to walk about in this room . . ." Then she leaves.

But in an Andre Serban production, with Irene Worth playing Lyubov, she did not exit. She paused, looked back, and began suddenly to circle, to "walk about" the room, her old nursery, just as her mother had done. At the door she paused again, a last look . . . and then another needed circling of the room, this time more quickly. Again at the door, again unable to cut herself loose, she now ran around the room for the third time, arms outstretched, weeping . . . and then out the door, running. Then the sound of the carriage leaving. A pause. Then the sound of an axe against a tree. A pause. Firs, a servant, enters. An old man, he has been forgotten. He sits, closes his eyes, perhaps forever. Pause. Then, as Chekhov writes, "A distant sound is heard that seems to come from the sky, the sound of a snapped string mournfully dying away. Stillness. Pause. Then the thud of the axe on a tree, again, again. Curtain." Oh, happy, oh, necessary pause.

THE AUDIENCE AND THE SERIOUSNESS OF WHAT'S FUNNY

Going from the sublime to the marvelously ridiculous, so that I— and you—don't take ourselves too seriously, the pause I love the most is Jack Benny's. Without his famous pause, he is inevitably crippled. Getting laughs is a very serious business indeed. Tom Stoppard said it best. Asked why he cared about whether a particular line gets a laugh, he answered: "I think of laughter as the sound of comprehension."[4]

Often, when an actor is offered a juicy part in a funny play, he begins to anticipate: "Oh, good—I get to make them laugh." But that should be the last time (at least until the last week of rehearsal) the actor should be concerned with getting laughs. From the first moment on stage, everything is serious. The situations, the character's

---

4. *The New Yorker*, March 7, 2011.

inner struggles, and the calamitous relationships are serious. George Abbott, the famous director of hit Broadway comedies in the first seven decades of the last century, cast the biggest comedians of his time and then forbade them to get a laugh with their famous "bits" for the first fifteen minutes of the play. ("What? What!?" they said. "Why? Why!?" But they did it.) Abbott wanted audiences to get involved in the story, to care about real people before the first banana peel fall-down.

The best comedies present a mirror so the audience can see "what fools we mortals be." The best comedians reveal themselves to us and reveal us to ourselves. The biggest laughs come from, "Oh, that happened to me! He's like me, I'm like that! I know about that!" or "That's just like my uncle!" The more the audience can empathize, the more they can experience a comedy in terms of their own personal banana peels, and the funnier the play will be.

That's true for any comedy—and even truer in a farce, in which the actor must take herself and the situation most seriously. As you rush to the telephone to get the news (no matter that you slip on that same banana peel on the way over), the news you receive must be unbelievably important—more important, even, than in a drama. The dilemma of the drama is serious. The dilemma of the tragedy is shatteringly serious. But the dilemma of a farce must be the most serious of all. The great farceurs, the great comedic actors, never let you see them thinking they are funny. For them, dilemmas are desperate.

Farce and tragedy are conjoined human experiences, separated in life, and on the stage, by the barest breath. What is funny and what is not is at best mysterious. In life, one person laughs uproariously, while another, annoyed, says, "What the hell are you laughing at?"

Or you, already late and in a great hurry to get yourself and your friend to the airport, can't get the car key to open the damn door. You're enraged, until you realize it's the wrong car. *Your* silver Civic is across the street. Everyone goes from big anger to big laugh fast. Even you.

On the stage, no matter what the author thought, no matter the certainty of the actors, finally it is only the audience who decides what's funny. How it decides what is and what is not laughworthy remains mysterious and complicated. In the theater, there are many different kinds of laughs. There is the idiot who laughs at the feed line of a joke and kills it for the rest of us. There is the "wrong" laugh at a serious moment, which, of course, we didn't want but which an audience says, "Sorry, but it is funny." Then the most fearful, getting "the bird," when the whole house laughs, not with you but at you.

Finally, there is the frustrating, unsatisfying, scattered giggling when what was wanted was the whole house to roar as one, what we call (vulgarly, for such a lovely moment) "a boff," when the laugh is not just a chuckle dribbling from one audience member to another, but when the playwright and actor have done something that creates a sudden burst, a shock wave, and everyone laughs at the same instant. Boff! To be at the center of that vortex is exhilarating. How to find that hidden explosion, that boff? Sometimes it's easy and comes without effort. Sometimes it's a sweet surprise, and sometimes it's exasperatingly difficult.

In a play I directed on Broadway in 1959 for the Theatre Guild (*Third Best Sport* by Eleanor Bayer and Leo Bayer), Celeste Holm could not get the big laugh where she knew—where we all knew—one lived. It was a big recognition joke line: "My God, you're a thief!" she says to her husband. She got only giggles. I tried to help. Nothing. Then the great producer Lawrence Langner, though an elderly man and no longer a theater titan, took me aside and said, "Michael, ask the playwright if she wouldn't mind changing the word 'thief' to 'crook.'" To humor him, the young man that I was gave in with some annoyance and spoke to the writer, who agreed to the change. I asked Celeste to change the word to "crook." That night she drew a thunderous boff. Why? Because the "f" in "thief" is heard little by little, but the "k" in "crook" is heard by all at the same instant. There's nothing quite like a hard "k" in the theater. (Maybe that's why four-letter words do so well.)

Another example: as a young actor, I auditioned for the famous Joshua Logan for the road company of *Mister Roberts*. After reading a funny line, Mr. Logan, sitting in the audience, called out, "Michael, don't smile at the end of the line." I wasn't smiling, I thought. I read it again. "Michael, you're still smiling." I read it again, grimly, I thought. "Michael, let your mouth stay open at the end of the line" (to me, a Method Actor!). I did, and I burst out laughing. I couldn't help it; it felt funny, even to me. "Deadpan," it's called, an odd name for a laugh-getter. But please don't mimic "mouth open." That external jaw drop will get you nowhere. Audiences have a nose for what's phony and what's funny. What was important for Logan and me was that now it seemed I took seriously my response to a foolish question and I gave him a serious answer without even the slightest intimation or awareness of what was funny.

STAYING WITHIN ONESELF: THE COMEDIC AND THE NON-COMEDIC

Comedy has many rewards for actors. But good actors, as well as comedians, yearn to play villains. These parts offer them the opportunity to live in their dark side publicly, to be unmasked behind the veneer of the character.

Villains are fun, but the joys of getting a laugh are incomparable, and they come from the actor's intimate relationship with the audience. Audience awareness in a comedy and audience awareness in a work that is noncomedic (all theater works are serious) need two very different approaches. While generalizing is often self-defeating, in this case it may be useful.

Performing in a comedy, the actor must pay attention to and learn from each individual audience. It is a glorious back and forth, give and withhold, in which every performance and each single moment becomes "for the first time." Each audience is either a good and willing partner or unresponsive or maybe sleepy (too much dinner, too much booze).

Rehearsing a comedy, however, is quite a different matter. As an actor rehearses, the audience should not be part of the equation. For the actor to discover what is funny, he must first discover what is most urgently serious. The behavior, the relationships, the developing of comic chops, must be an internal process, completely removed from audience concern or what you or anyone else thinks is funny. In rehearsal, up to the last moment, whether it's low comedy or Oscar Wilde, what every comedy wants from the actor is the total immersion in situation, relationship, and character, and then, perhaps, finding "funny" within it. There is such a thing as comedy-truth. Trust it. Comic integrity, finding truth in "what's funny," is sometimes harder than finding truth in *Oedipus*. It is what the rehearsal should be for.

The actor-audience relationship in a "straight" play is most different from performing in a comedy. A play that tries to confront a life close up, without a comedic remove, demands of the actor an absolute distancing from being watched. To exaggerate, if an actor were to go through an entire performance so involved in the circumstances of the play that he was unaware there were watchers (it's not possible, nor even preferable), that would seem enviable. It is, after all, what the actor wants—to be so caught up in the imaginary world that nothing interferes. Not only does this never happen, but when the actor is working really well, he wants to be open to the whole universe. The good actor refuses to hold herself apart from what is happening now, even when it seems counter to the situation or the relationship. She demands of herself that she live in the now, the present moment—I mean the visceral pleasure of being totally present, no longer acting, yet completely inside the character and within the world of the play, in front of hundreds of people.

Of course at moments the actor will feel the audience's response, whether he wants to or not. He will sense their quiet, or their restlessness, will be aware they are part of this moment. He will also know that for long stretches he will forget them. The "fourth wall" will materialize when he is concentrated on the other actors, when he is committed to what must be done. I recognize that creating the fourth wall can be valuable in creating a strong sense of "place," of theatrical geography, but it should not be used to separate the actor from the audience. Do not maintain a fourth wall; don't shut the audience out. They will emerge and go away, emerge and go away, but they are always an essential part of the triangle.

Essential they are, but never try to please them. Wanting them, needing them, to love you is a disease that results in conventional, even vulgar, acting. Attempt to please no one—not even the director! The director and the audience will be most satisfied when the actor-artist is concerned with solving the creative problem. And never ask, "Does it read?"

Stars, if they choose, can break the fourth wall or ignore it when dealing with a crass audience. Katharine Hepburn, appearing on Broadway, was once presented with someone who came in late and fussily took her seat in one of the front rows. Hepburn stopped the play, turned to the woman, and said, in effect, "We're just going to wait for you." John Barrymore, playing Hamlet, apparently was afflicted in one performance by an incessant cougher in one of the boxes. Interrupting his performance, Barrymore looked at the offender and said, "Throw that barking seal a fish!" Then he resumed his work. Hugh Jackman, in a performance of *A Steady Rain* in New York, became so irritated by cell phones and even cameras flashing that he stopped in mid-sentence and remonstrated with the audience before he could recover his concentration and resume. Perhaps an extreme of this reaction was when, in 2015, Patti LuPone grabbed the phone out of the hand of a texting audience member. Only stars can do that, of course, and then only when they are seriously bothered. I think stars react this way not only to rid themselves (and their otherwise friendly audience) of an annoying distraction, but also because they want to be totally present and not to live two lives (the actor-life and the character-life). The other actors notice the disturbance, breathe, and choose to continue.

Art is choice. The actor is available to anything and aware of everything. Then the actor can choose to ignore, to hide, to reveal. To pay attention. To learn from the choices and change, or choose to play it as planned. To become an actor-artist takes thousands of hours and many years of practice. Learning when and how to encourage the flow of imagination, the intuitive thrust, and when to gently deny it, is an important part of what we mean by "technique."

TECHNIQUE: WHAT DOES IT ENCOMPASS?

Technique is how to live truthfully on the stage. Everything the actor does is technique. Technique is "how" we do what we do. Too often it is understood only as relating to the voice, physical abilities and accomplishments, and externals relating to style. In fact, it is useful to recognize that an actor's technique encompasses all the inner workings of the actor's art as well as the externals. The internal and external ways of the actor's work are intricately entwined. Technique should never be thought of as the mechanics of acting, nor should the art of acting ever be viewed mechanistically.

The development of a technique, learning the craft, finding personal solutions, gives great existential pleasure. Finding a new way, a never-tried-before way, to solve a problem that a movie demands, that the television industry requires, or that a complicated character presents—the challenges, the difficulties, then the solution suddenly or slowly revealed—is the heart and soul of the creative act.

No single book can describe how all actors should work. Every actor develops his own technique, his own way, stimulated and prodded by provocative systems, good teachers, watching, listening, staying curious—to which add all of life's experiences: the trials and errors, successes and failures, and, most of all, working as an actor. Out of all that comes a technique, and it cannot be labeled with somebody else's name, not even exemplary ones like Meisner, Adler, Strasberg, Hagen, not even Stanislavski. A good actor's own name will be attached to her work.

TECHNIQUE AND TRICKS

"Yes, I have tricks in my pocket, I have things up my sleeve," says Tom in the first line of Tennessee Williams's *The Glass Menagerie*. Tom (Tennessee) is speaking about the writer. All artists have "tricks," and that includes the actor. Of course we have tricks. Deep, psychological, internal tricks, as well as character-revealing and laugh-getting tricks.

Good actors try to work with intellectual clarity as they grapple with the writer's driving ambition—even before they deal with the story. Actors work consciously as well as intuitively. They will work with their own inner connections and with what comes from the other actors. Inevitably, the play will make demands that cannot be solved even by the most cohesive, moment-to-moment living-through of the rehearsal. Sometimes the most incisive results are based on a preponderance of the actor's experiences, his knowledge, stored in the memory of brain and muscle, of what has worked in similar situations.

Actors also learn more superficial, but necessary, ways of problem-solving. Making a good entrance and a good exit can be important. They know, for instance, how to give audiences time to laugh and when to start the next line—before the laugh is quite over. Actors learn tricks that are creative and truthful.

For example, one way to work on a character who stammers is to choose just one letter on which to stutter. The choice of which letter, or even which word, will depend on whether the play is comedic or serious. The choice may even be based on psychology: "m" for "mother," or "s" for "sex."

A character affected by alcohol (I don't like the designation "drunk" because it encourages the drunk cliché) will find that certain parts of the body are more affected than others. Alcohol affects muscles, and that affects balance. Trying to articulate an important idea, the muscles of the mouth cannot control the tongue and the lips; the diaphragm, which is a muscle, can become incapable of producing the required breath. Some characters won't even be aware that the alcohol is affecting them until they try to stand and the room circles. Every character is different when she has alcohol in her system. What the author writes will define for the actor where and how much the body is affected.

Always, one wants the specific, never the general. When a cabdriver says he's tired, it's his butt and his back that hurt. A computer geek will have carpal tunnel syndrome and bleary eyes from his time in front of a screen. A longshoreman will have sore shoulders and biceps—muscle-tiredness from lifting. Hungover? Fever? Tired? Choose a particular physical affect and then, most important, try to overcome that obstacle to achieve what the character wants. Never act the illness, the alcohol, or the pain. Place the pain, alcohol, or fever somewhere in the body, then climb the stairs, dance the dance, catch the cab.

Nowhere is a more delicate technique needed than when dealing with a truthful emotional response. When a playwright indicates that a character weeps—assuming the actor's ability to create the strong internal response that causes the tears that the author suggests—the character, like all humans, should try not to cry. Resist the trap of trying to make tears. On the other hand, if the actor cannot find the internal truth when the text dictates upset, surprise, a shock to the system, he can immediately change his breathing pattern; changing the breath changes the internal and external response. The actor should find a response in the body to this external attack—an ache in the stomach, a sudden pain in the shoulder, a pressure on the temples.

Any discussion of theatrical storytelling should always include the great value of choosing the non-illustrative physical action to help reveal relationship and situational truth. If on page seven you are told, "You're drinking too much," on page six, finish your drink and then finish hers, or put the bottle away. If on page fifteen your character says, "It's cold in here," do nothing because on page fourteen, you already got up and put on a sweater, or felt the radiator, or closed the window. (No illustrative rubbing your hands on page fifteen, please.) In both examples, the audience will be more engaged, will be working with you because of the earlier physical action that complements the later text.

No trick, no tool (a better word) is more useful than the magical "as if." In life, we speak using "as if" all the time. For instance, we seem to need to describe how dangerous a situation was by saying, figuratively, "it was as if I walked into a nest of vipers." The actor takes this casual remark and turns it into physical and psychological behavior—truthful, but never illustrative: "I will play this moment as if I just won the World Series"; "I will play this entrance as if I am returning from a funeral"—in plays that have nothing to do with sports or funerals. Why not just use what's written on the page? Sometimes the play's situation alone does not create the heightened concern that the theater wants. If the character is about to enter a room filled with potential danger or menace, the actor can choose to behave as if she is entering a cage of lions without a whip. Such a choice gives the actor a heightened sense of danger. It stimulates the imaginative process and creates specific, unconventional tempo and behavior. The actor chooses as much or as little of the developed behavior as she thinks is artistically useful. But tell no one what you're doing—certainly not the director or the other actors. It is for you—to tickle your imagination.

Every good craftsman knows that tools are for problem-solving. Actors have tools that are used in almost every job. Others are used rarely. No new problem to solve? No new tools are necessary. We have tools to externalize an internal truth, to create character, to particularize relationships, to develop the situation, to explore the external environment, the "where" you are (your place or his place? Is it hot, cold, early, late . . . ?). Be curious about with which of these questions the writer is most concerned. Remain curious. Keep asking questions. Answers come when you're not looking.

Every craftsman loves his own special collection of tools, tucked away in the suitcase, just in case. But perhaps the most useful element of an actor's technique is to know when to leave yourself alone, when to do nothing, when to allow your intuition, your imagination, and the momentum of the play to move you forward. The experienced actor recognizes those moments when he reads a play, or even a scene, and says, "I know about this, I'm going to leave it alone. I'm not going to think, I'm not going to decide, I'm not going to question; I'm just going to be present. There's enough that seems to be happening as I read it for me to leave myself alone." That's a very good response, and the experienced actor does just that. That same actor, with another play, reads it and recognizes that "I don't know a lot about this. Is that what this is? I'm going to have to do some work here. I'm going to have to really dig around. *Where is that suitcase?*" It will take some craft to bring that part of himself, that particular piece that he doesn't know a lot about or hasn't used in his work before.

A technique is not static, not unchanging. A mature actor's way of working is a living thing—always in flux, always ready to surprise or even to disappoint. It will seem to have its own life. The tool that worked yesterday won't work today. An element of craft, reliable for years, suddenly becomes lifeless. On another day, and after many performances, suddenly and without warning a connection is made between two actors who will be dazzled and be miraculously present in a new truth, in front of many strangers.

As the actor grows and develops, so does her technique and her muscles. New understandings come to the rescue with lovely surprises and new tools. One thing that never changes is the actor's need for orientation.

ORIENTATION

Orientation is what we humans do, consciously or not, at the beginning of every new experience. Exits, entrances, new friends, changes in old friends, changes in the weather—we notice. And then ignore, or go back and get a sweater.

My dog Sam paid serious attention to orientation. Sam taught me much about acting. When I would give voice to a momentary dilemma and one of Sam's ears went up, I would continue, if only half seriously, sharing with him a real problem. His listening was intent and relaxed. There was no scratching or moving around. He almost convinced me that he understood what I was talking about. I began to watch what Sam did when he was hungry or when he wanted to "go" urgently. The specifics of his behavior depended on the importance of his need. He always pursued what he wanted until I gave it to him. My dog understood the concept of an "action" and of finding different ways to accomplish it.

One of the important things Sam did was practice orientation. When we went into a new place, when we visited a friend's apartment

133

for the first time, he would circle the apartment, sniffing, looking, orienting. Even when we would return home after a walk and before he settled down, he would check out the room—he would orient.

Humans have the same impulse. We orient continually—with every new beginning, with every new person, in every new space. Even when I come home at the end of a day, without thinking I send out a probe: "Betty?" I call to my wife. If there is no answer, I send out another probe, louder. If there still isn't an answer, I stop checking the mail and I look for Betty. I have been orienting, just as Sam oriented when we would return from a walk. I orient with almost all of my senses, just like Sam—my nose, ears, eyes, even my skin. An unusual odor? An unexplained sound? A chair out of place? A chill? Or is everything in order?

Notice what you do the next time you enter a subway car or a bus. You check the space. You notice where you will sit and where you won't, where sits danger and where sits possible pleasure. If there is an odor, you will notice it. We don't think about it; it's what we do. Show up at a cocktail party, and even when there is a strong "want," an important reason to be there (to meet that agent, let's say), your first thirty seconds there are rich with orientation: "Where a friendly face? What's that awful perfume? Damn, only white wine again." Your sensory equipment provides information on which to act before you find the host (and the agent). Orientation. Usually unconscious, but sometimes very conscious, it is the beginning of almost every new human (or, for that matter, animal) experience.

It is important for the actor to include orienting, no matter how urgent the "want." When "meeting" a new person, a new food, a new place, or a new dilemma, actors must orient. The actor should think of orienting as part of his unconscious behavior, much like my dog.

It is intuitive, habitual, logical. In every entrance, be open to orientation. No matter how strong the chosen action, no matter the immediacy, make sure you have appetite and room to discover the new, the unexpected change. This is what it means to be totally present. What you encounter may change the "how" by which you accomplish what must be done.

ENTRANCES AND EXITS

Entrances and exits mark the hours, days, and years of our lives—and that is true of our lives in the theater, as well. On the stage, every entrance must be treated with respect. In the world of the play, the need to enter the imaginary world and its emotional climate, the required physical energy, must be present long before the door is opened. And exits often begin pages before you say "goodnight."

Pay attention to every entrance, not just the first big, sometimes heavy, sometimes "funny" entrance, but each succeeding one, whether simple or complicated. It means a total commitment to where your character is coming from, what she's doing on the way over, and what she wants when she gets there. Each entrance will need a different, specific preparation.

The nineteenth-century critic George Henry Lewes reported that the great actor William Charles Macready, playing Shylock, after discovering his beloved daughter has been spirited away to marry a Christian, prepared for the entrance by "cursing, sotto voce, and shaking violently a ladder fixed against the wall," and then rushing onstage.[5]

---

5. George Henry Lewes, *On Actors and the Art of Acting* (New York: Henry Holt & Co., 1878), 44.

That same century also featured shamefully grand entrances— shameful, but fun. Great stars knew what audiences wanted in an entrance and they gave it to them. One was called "The Center Door Fancy": large double doors, up-center, in the middle of the stage. All the other actors in the room, knowing that "she's coming," stand with their backs to the audience. Suddenly the double doors are flung open, and down she comes, often trailing a fur. Center Door Fancy—audiences loved it, expected it, and now, thank goodness, have forgotten it.

Now we do things differently. Every entrance must be enriched by the life before and the life going forward. Make it specific, make it detailed, make it truthful. In some cases, make it hugely theatrical, if that's the truth of the character or the situation. In *The Shadow Box*, by Michael Cristofer, note Beverly's entrance and you'll know what hugely theatrical means.

Even more significant in the theater and in our lives are exits. Think about your own life: often happy to leave, miserable when you are gone, or wanting to stay but forced to go. Conflict and resolution. Theater.

Jimmy Durante, comedy star of the early twentieth century, said it best when he famously spoke-sang, "Did you ever have the feeling that you wanted to go when you still had the feeling that you wanted to stay?" It's on the Internet. It's iconic. And very funny. In many exits in the theater, which are prompted by the stage direction "he exits," the character may well feel like Jimmy Durante. There are exits sad, exits painful, exits mysterious. A good example: Malvolio's entrance and immediate exit, right before the final curtain in Shakespeare's *Twelfth Night*.

Some exits need a different solution. In *Light Up the Sky*, a rather foolish director is fired by the producer—a man named Mr. Black. Moss Hart, the playwright, has given the fired director an excellent laugh line and a great exit for the actor. Speechless at the injustice that has been visited upon him and desperate to recover his dignity, the fired director walks to the door and just before he exits says, "Mr. Black, I think . . . you stink!"

Comedy technique demands internal and external choices. First, the actor must find the strongest internal need to come up with the best verbal weapon to respond to this terrible mistreatment as he moves to the door. Still searching for a face-saver, the actor opens the door and with his hand on the doorknob, turns back and says, "Mr. Black . . . I think . . . you stink," and exits, slamming the door (bang!). That quick door slam after the line triggers a big laugh. Saying that line brilliantly (after all, the writer has given the actor two hard Ks) and then walking to the door only gets giggles.

When such an exit is done properly, it becomes a gift to the audience. We give them a deeply satisfying belly laugh. Of course, they thank you and applaud on the exit. Anything less would be ungrateful. Learning the "how" of a good exit is part of an actor's technique.

In Shakespeare's *The Winter's Tale*, there is a famous—and still controversial—exit in Act III, Scene 3. The script says that Antigonus "exit[s], pursued by a bear."[6] There has been no prior mention of a bear. I have my own theory: The organizer of this piece of stage business (perhaps Shakespeare himself), watching a poor actor making a painfully slow exit, perhaps more than once, ordered him to "Go! Go! Quick! Go!" And finally, exasperated: "Go as if you're being

---

6. William Shakespeare, *The Winter's Tale: Second Series*, ed. J. H. P. Pafford (London: Thomson Learning, 2006), 69.

pursued by a bear!" Some stealthy plagiarist, hiding in the back of the theater, head down, writing furiously (there to "steal" the play for another theater or a pirate publisher), hearing "pursued by a bear," added it to the play's text, and it has come down to us this way. (Of course, there are other explanations, but I like mine best.)

HOW MUCH SHOULD ONE PERFORMANCE BE LIKE THE LAST ONE?

The rehearsal establishes for the actors a road on which the performances travel. The road includes the obvious aspects concerning physical presence and the essentials of a relationship but also nuances, subtleties, and tempos. Inevitably, moments get repeated. Should those moments, even the best of them, be locked in? How much should the actor allow them to change during performance? Where and to what degree must they remain the same? Where and how much must they change? Everyone would agree that, night after night, it has to seem as if what is happening has never happened before. What can the actor do to create that "for the first time" experience for each new audience?

What is most important is to allow the potential for differences. When the night begins, even though the stage manager has the journey written down to the smallest detail, you the actor—secretly perhaps—must be open to change, must be able to respond to a slightly different sound from the audience, to an oddly deeper response from another actor or, more importantly, from yourself.

The watchers and the watched are involved in a living experience. Yes, the text is the same (exactly, please); even the physical moves are essentially the same. But as the play develops, performance after performance, some wholly new organism emerges. It is alive, changing, growing—always the same and always somehow different, from one moment to the next. The roots of your performance should sink deeper, the limbs should become stronger. It must not resemble a machine moving along exactly the same as it did yesterday and the night before.

But what is "the same"? At what point can the playwright say, "Wait a minute! I wrote a play about a man who loves a woman. He cares about her. He wants to help her. What I saw tonight is a play about somebody who is self-involved and sorry he ever met this woman." You do not want to do that and won't do it if you stay connected to the integrity of the playwright's event. But what can change, what must change, is the depth of desire to "help her," the way of helping, seeing her differently night to night, one night foolish, another night needy. Her need and how she expresses it can change night to night, as must your response. Two good actors will play the same notes but will allow the tempo, the urgency, the inference, the depth of their understanding of each other to change.

As in life, the expression of a relationship will vary in intensity, humor, or passion. In any given scene, in any given performance, some truth hidden in the play's run thus far can suddenly be revealed to the actor, and even to the playwright. We would like the writer to say, "Whoa, that's wonderful, that's true, I didn't even know that was in that moment!" Not only do we want the writer to say it, we want the actor to declare: "I found something tonight, in the 110th performance, that makes me better understand the play."

On the famous other hand, Harold Clurman, wise director and critic, was about to revisit a play he had directed about a month after it had opened. Asked, "What are you going to do tonight?" he replied, "I'm going to take out the improvements."

Yes, actors can have an inspired moment, but we cannot always have perspective on our place in the journey. That is true in life and in acting. In 1958, I saw two performances in New York of John Osborne's *The Entertainer*. Laurence Olivier, then fifty-one, was playing Archie Rice, an over-the-hill music hall performer. Joan Plowright, Olivier's wife, was Archie's daughter. I saw it on two consecutive nights. In one scene, Plowright is on a ladder decorating a Christmas tree. Olivier climbs up, handing her decorations and talking to her. The first night I saw it, he held on to her hand and kissed it. The next night, he not only held on to her hand, he put her thumb in his mouth. Plowright just ripped it away. Kissing his daughter on the hand only hints obliquely at an incestuous feeling. What Olivier did the second night made it undeniable—the moment put a hot white light on his incestuous feelings. In an interview with David Susskind in 1960, the actress Vivian Leigh said of Olivier, "Larry was never the same" from one performance to the next. "It was always different. You never knew what he would do." Note, please: that she is speaking of an actor of genius, working after thirty years of practice, who has earned the right to extemporize.

Some changes are conscious and some—even major ones—occur unconsciously. There is another Olivier story, perhaps apocryphal, but illuminating and instructive nonetheless. After he had given an especially rich performance, a close theatrical friend went to his dressing room to congratulate him. He found Olivier pacing in his dressing room, still in makeup and costume, absolutely beside himself. "What's the matter?" the friend asked, "You were so wonderful tonight!" "I know, I know," Olivier roared, "but I don't know how I did it!"

REPEATING THE INSPIRED OR REQUIRED MOMENT

Acting is easy . . . and bad acting is very easy. There's a lot of it. High school acting, which is full of joy, excitement, brio, and absolute certainty, continues into some colleges and even into the profession. Then there is acceptable acting. It isn't very difficult, either; in fact it's often well paid in various media. It is based on the expectation, and the acceptance, of what is conventional. It is concerned with pleasing someone other than yourself. It is part of the culture of "How am I doing? Does it read?"—of pleasing your friends, your family, and later the director, the producer.

Then there are those times when, even in the media world of hurry-up storytelling or the hobbyist in the community theater, an actor, without knowing how or why, inexplicably overcomes the "acceptable," transcends the mediocre, and tumbles into a new universe—at least once.

For the professional actor, to whom such a moment can happen more often, it is thrilling, even stunning, when that deeper fulfillment of the play's vision arrives. In this sudden awakening, the actor is totally present, focused, breathing, completely available to his internal and external world: in the zone. It can happen in performance or in rehearsal, early or late. Perhaps some word or phrase in the text that has never quite landed before turns the key. Sometimes, the other actor provides the spark. Or a secret, unexpected connection to the actor's own life suddenly emerges.

It is then that the actor realizes that this inspired moment, this deeply anchored involvement, can be difficult to re-experience, performance after performance, or take after take—not the result, not

141

the end product, but the cause, the kick that released it. Not only is that acting problem not easy, but like all good and serious acting, it can also be toilsome and emotionally elusive. Re-experiencing the inspired moment is perhaps the most difficult problem confronting the actor, and it is only with craft and after years of practice that answers begin to develop. The inspired moment is the gift with which your talent and intuition surprise you.

Then there is the required moment, agreed upon by the actor and the director, richly conceived and delivered in the course of rehearsals as the best of all possible ways to reveal the author's intention. But the required moment, too, can be most difficult to accomplish truthfully, night after night. How can the actor repeat these moments with the freshness, inevitability, and truth they had the first time they happened (especially in a theater in which the happy possibility of a long run is always the hope)? There is no "this solves everything" answer.

What you will find is this: acting is doing. Whether with the body or with language or with both, there is something that must be done. If you have had an inspired moment that was internally motivated and externally realized, and you need to find it again, go back to what you were doing. Stay away from what you were feeling, from watching the feelings, and concentrate instead on listening to and affecting your partner. Become fully absorbed in a physical activity that reflects an internal need. Stay as far away as you can from the hope of recreating the emotion of that moment. The more you are focused and the deeper your concentration on what must be done, the more possible it becomes to stop judging yourself, to stop watching yourself, so that your intuition can rouse from its sleep, see that you are busy elsewhere, help you rediscover what sparked the inspired moment, and thereby allow it to reemerge. The intuition doesn't shout; it whispers. Concentrate on what happened directly before that moment and forget about what is about to happen.

The goal is to re-experience, but never to repeat. The strong connection to a particular moment will always change. Welcome the change. It will become deeper or shallower, with pain or with more humor. The good actor accepts what she is given at the moment it occurs, the experience of the now—not looking for yesterday—of being totally present, breathing. Living in the moment as you receive it is what the best acting is about. If the moment is gone, then accept that it's gone, and that something else will come up. Remember that even a magnificently talented and experienced actor like Olivier cannot always know. The best acting is a mystery.

MYSTERIES AND PUZZLES

Unconventional, surprising, and transformative acting is a mystery, a tantalizing mystery. Enjoy it. Respect it as you watch it and most especially as you do it. And as you do it, know the destination but leave open and changeable how to get there. Mysteries reveal themselves slowly, unexpectedly. Puzzles—crossword or jigsaw puzzles—have absolute answers: the right word or the right piece. Too often, theater workers treat acting as a puzzle and thereby deny its mystery. They ask for absolute answers, arrange things neatly, and offer performances that lack heat and spontaneity.

The opposite of demanding absolute answers is the extraordinarily useful "I don't know." To say, "I don't know anything about most things in the universe in which I live" is to make room to be surprised and to experience the next small moment of enlightenment. Those three words—"I don't know"—are the great door opener. I am talking about the rehearsal and, at times, even the performance. Rehearsals are about "I don't know, I'll find out." Rehearse to discover; rehearse to test; rehearse *Hamlet* for Hamlet to be surprised. Readers of a play have only an imagined Ophelia. In rehearsal and in performance, actors have a flesh-and-blood Ophelia—a changeable, silly, sexy, foolish, or desperately childlike one-time playmate. Hamlet, what will you do or say, as she approaches? "I don't know" is the wonderfully creative answer. After many go-throughs of that scene, the actor makes an artistic choice (art is, after all, choice) but always leaves open the impulse, the sudden loving impulse, for instance, to kiss her before sending her off to the nunnery. One of the joys of acting is the living-through, the not knowing—of oneself surprised!

In a long run of a play, it is indeed hard to maintain the mystery. You have opened every door, looked into every corner, tried things nine different ways. Nevertheless, when the curtain goes up, the actor (and the audience) should feel anything is possible. If you are too comfortable, the audience will be too comfortable and tend to doze. If you know where everything is going to land, the audience will get there ahead of you and their playbills will begin to rustle. But when the actor stays edgy, explores alternative actions, tests the opposites—that can be exciting, provocative, tastier. Audiences smell risk, and they respond to actors who have a life beyond the words and beneath the surface.

STAGE FRIGHT

Earlier, I wrote about the danger and the pleasure of standing in the wings, waiting for the word, "Curtain." Pleasure. Excitement. And also fear, unreasonable fear. Stage fright.

In 1944, I was training in Fort Benning, Georgia, as an enlistee in the parachute troops. We had to climb a perpendicular ladder some fifty feet high that ended in a rickety wooden platform. The climb up the ladder, hand over hand, seemed endless. Once on the platform, we had to hook a wire to a harness similar to a pair of suspenders, step to the edge, and then jump into space. I stood on the platform, feeling nothing on my back but knowing that the wire that stretched from my suspenders to a pole and pulley contraption would keep me, by a mere fifteen feet, from smashing into the ground. I was sweating, my heart pounding, my mouth dry, as I waited for the jump cue. Suddenly, I experienced a surge of excitement, even pleasure, at being on the edge of something dangerous, at being alive, being challenged. I entered into space. An entrance I'll never forget.

My leap into space that day has always seemed like the first entrance in a new play. My brain knew I would not smash into the ground, but my psyche wasn't convinced—a bit like stage fright. It took courage. But the actor's leap in his entrance, knowing that in so doing he will be revealed, will be vulnerable, will be available to ridicule, even hostility, that leap is really brave.

Stage fright at some level can affect all actors. Nor does it have any respect for years on the stage or even the proper preparation of craft. Only the ability to concentrate on something other than oneself, the choice of a preparation that demands sharp focus, consuming concentration, can begin to lessen the fear. That, and remembering to breathe. Enjoy the accelerated heartbeat, even the dry mouth. Accept the challenge, the excitement, the triumph of being alive and present.

Chapter 14
On Camera versus Onstage

Today, there is a sense that on-camera acting needs something other than what the theater actor already has. That is not true. Film acting, with all its technological demands, still wants what the actor brings to the workplace, wherever it is: talent, sensibility, insight, risk. The actor-work, the craftwork, is the same whatever the medium. Of course, there are new challenges, but the one element that does not, and must not, change—no matter the technology—is the actor's internal, developed sense of truth. A theater actor working in film uses acquired theater skills and adapts them to solve the challenges of a film script. A film will not ask a good actor for anything he does not have. Actors understand technical demands.

Consider the technical challenges of working in the theater. Changes in how the actor works come first from the venue. Large or small, proscenium or in the round, inside or outside, the actor must adapt. An actor in a one hundred–seat house is able to be truthful with quiet intimacy. In a one thousand–seat house, she must still be able to share herself in an intimate moment but must do so with more breath, more body, and she must enlarge her emotional lens to reach the back of the house. But the essential desire to experience and thereby to reveal and to illuminate internal truth does not change.

An actor working "in the round" must technically share himself front, back, and center, equally, and sometimes arbitrarily. Another actor has learned how to live creatively with the physical world the set designers have given her. Should she now be asked to act on a bare stage—no props, no furniture—she will adapt.

Creating every moment, fully realized, before the character moves on to the next fully realized moment is what makes a satisfying performance in live theater. But the ability of the actor to develop one moment at a time is also at the core of film acting. Because films are shot without emotional continuity and out of sequence (the death scene is on the first day of shooting, the romantic first encounter on the last), what the good actor is left with, what he must be able to accomplish, truthfully, is one moment at a time. But there is one major difference between film and theater storytelling. The live theater gives you the continuity of the play to arrive at the emotional trauma. Film acting gives the actor no such momentum; he must be prepared to create just that moment—without the benefit of what has immediately come before—again and again, and then again. In filmmaking, the medium does not help you move step by step to a climax.

Greta Garbo is on the telephone in an early film, *Grand Hotel*. She creates an extraordinary and emotionally truthful long moment . . . scene . . . take. Perhaps right before that moment, she was sitting in a chair, quietly sipping coffee or speaking to the makeup woman. Then someone said, "We're ready for you, Miss Garbo." Now she moves to the set, breathes, and hears, "Action!" And that painful moment,

147

yearning, emotionally needy, begins. She is spellbinding. Her ability to create that moment with such effortless believability takes our breath away. I do not know how Ms. Garbo prepared, but I know that she had her own way of reaching deep within herself to ignite the moment as she picked up the telephone. Her craftwork, the preparation for such a highly charged moment, is the same for the stage actor waiting in the wings to make her entrance.

Much has been said about the external needs of the director in shooting a scene. A director wants only what he wants in the frame. There are technical demands in film acting that must be accomplished. When a close-up is called for, too often the very good stage actor will be told, "You're moving around too much. Stay still." That (stupid) instruction can undermine good acting. What is necessary to accomplish what the director of photography needs from the actor is less casual movement. To accomplish this, there must be greater intensity and urgency and a deeper ongoing inner life. Urgency, the sharp attention on the other, is what correctly inhibits casual movement.

In addition, the actor must hit a mark on the floor, or find her key light, or look deep into her lover's eyes as she looks into the camera lenses. Creative actors, the best of the profession, find ways to solve technical problems like these without any loss of inner truth or involvement in the moment. In the theater, the actor is asked to watch a nonexistent tennis match or to live through an earthquake. On film, the actor may have to fight with a computer robot or act with special effects that will be added in postproduction. Making the imaginary real is what the actor does, whether in front of the camera or onstage. Maintaining personal truth in the face of complicated technology is essential.

Even the simple technical demand of hitting a mark can be accomplished imaginatively without violating a sense of personal truth. Spencer Tracy, when asked to hit his mark, to move from point A to point B so that the camera could follow him and he would remain in focus, would sometimes look down at the ground, finding his mark. He made no split between character and actor. In the finished film, it was as if the character had his eyes downcast, pondering some thought. In reality, Tracy was looking for his mark.

The stage actor can likewise be confronted with the technical demands of hitting a mark and finding her light. *The Rainmaker*, a play by N. Richard Nash, was directed on Broadway by a fine actor and director, Joe Anthony, and it starred Geraldine Page, who was known for her sometimes excessive (and endearing) physical mannerisms, so much so that at one point during rehearsals, Mr. Anthony famously called out from the back of the theater, "Gerry, don't just do something, stand there!" In that play, at the end of a series of highly emotional scenes, Anthony asked Page to stand absolutely still. He wanted to black out every light except for her one spotlight, which held on her for five seconds before it went out, after which Ms. Page moved into the next scene. Some time later, I asked Joe whether Ms. Page ever missed her mark. "No, never."

Though the essential craft that the actor brings to the work is the same for the camera as it is for the theater, there are, still, distinctions. Chief among them, of course, is the presence in theater of the live audience. The live theater demands of the actor a living-through of a two-hour journey, experiencing the beginning, middle, and end—every night different, every night the same. It is exhausting and exhilarating, and in the great parts, the actor has the play itself, the story, to support and maintain him. A theater-trained actor playing Medea, Willy Loman, or even Peter Pan is like a marathoner; the runner understands the changing physical and psychological needs, mile after mile, the rest places, and the move to the finish. The practiced film actor, the very best, is more like a champion of the one hundred–yard or even four hundred–yard dash, who sits waiting. The race is called. She walks to the starting point. "On your mark. Get set. Go!" She sprints to the finish. It is truly an extraordinary achievement, just like an actor doing a scene on a film set. The actor-artist must be ready for both the marathon and the dash.

Chapter 15
The Always-Present Internal Improvisation

Internal improvisation, in life as well as on the stage, is that only-in-the-mind conversation, always present but silent, sometimes monitored, sometimes running free-form, often enriched with hidden humor, at other times pregnant with barely masked anger.

In life, this inner conversation is sparked unconsciously, unplanned, mostly undirected, and coming from only one ego. On the stage, however, there are always two egos: the created character speaking loudly and authoritatively with its own subtext, confidently moving forward; and the working actor's own small, secret voice—complaining, judging himself and others, rarely complimenting. Two alternating egos, each creating its own inner conversation, sometimes at odds, sometimes in tandem. The most annoying and anti-craft dilemma this presents can be called "The Two-Voice Disease": the actor-voice and the character-voice both existing separately onstage. These two arias should become one, and that one voice, even that secret negating, judging voice, should become part of the wonderfully imagined character's subtext.

How often in life do we think, "Damn, I said that badly," or "What was I going to say? I forget." Invite, even encourage, every thought and every experience once the stage lights are up and welcome them into your imagined world.

Of course, the actor wants this spontaneous inner talk-a-thon to come directly from the character's wants, but sometimes this inner aria emerges only from the actor's own fears, displeasures, or from sudden gifts, wanted or unwanted, that come from other actors. It is the ability of the fully present and trained actor to encourage real thought, private thought, truthful and unconventional, no matter its origin, that allows talent to define character. (In *On the Waterfront*, Marlon Brando, so hurt, so in pain, riding in the cab with his gangster brother, expels an unwritten "Oh Charlie, oh Charlie" out of his inner monologue. That unwritten, actor-improvised line encapsulates Brando's character and makes that scene memorable. So said the director, Elia Kazan.)[7]

Not every situation in a play evokes such a fraught inner conversation. Often this silent monologue simply extends the meaning and the logic of the written line, and again as in life, it lies there, quiescent. At other times, it can seem annoyingly digressive. Never mind. Good actors welcome and even encourage all internal improvisation to be present and visible and sometimes even allow it to affect behavior. They allow it to make changes—not to what is wanted in a scene but to how that want is pursued.

A strong line of action, arrived at and clarified during rehearsals, wants continuing spontaneity, surprises, the extraordinariness of reality rather than conventional naturalness. In rehearsal as well

---

7. Jeff Young, *Kazan: The Master Director Discusses His Films* (New York: Newmarket Press, 1999), 168.

as in performance, the actor welcomes the sudden emergence of a new way to accomplish what must be done. It can also be worthless, wrong, and, it is hoped, never to be seen again. Creative work wants the unexpected, not for its own sake, but rather for those sudden emerging moments that, when they occur, seem absolutely right and inevitable.

IV.

The Continuing Profession

Chapter 16:
Why an Actor's Laboratory?

At least since the Civil War, there have been theater schools in this country led by well-known theater artists. Most often, they were created for the beginning actor, intended to introduce a student to specific approaches, including Dalcroze Eurhythmics, pantomime, diction, and the "Spoken Word," or to teach the "rules" of stage behavior—all now out-of-date techniques from the nineteenth century. The professional laboratory for the developed actor to continue his growth was not an accepted part of the American tradition. But in the 1920s, the expatriate Russian artists Richard Boleslavsky and Maria Ouspenskaya created a workshop they called the American Laboratory Theatre, designed to explore the work of Stanislavski.

Professional actors, directors, even critics and producers, were eager to explore these new methods. For most of them, the experience was transformational. Years later, many of them were instrumental in transforming theater training in the United States, but the concept of professionals continuing to study was still not widely accepted. It was only in the mid-1930s, with the excitement generated by the work of the Group Theatre and with Michael Chekhov (nephew of Anton) beginning to teach in this country, that actors more generally were drawn to continuing their professional training.

In the late 1930s and into 1940, when the Group Theatre ended, there was much interest in understanding its way of working, and Lee Strasberg, Stella Adler, and Sanford Meisner (major members of the Group) introduced ongoing classes for professional actors—and thereby changed American theater. The advent of the Actors Studio in 1947 (the same year that Uta Hagen began her classes) made continuing study an accepted part of an actor's career. Some actors began to see the value of a professional acting class; others laughed at such time-wasting foolishness. Many actors still do.

What is such a professional acting class? And is it a class? Why would a mature actor feel she needs such a class or laboratory?

Obviously, to keep oneself in shape is important. Acting is a physically demanding profession. Like the dancer going to the barre most days, the singer doing vocal exercises each day, or even the marathoner who runs five to ten miles four times a week, the actor needs to keep tuned—not only physically but internally tuned as well, especially while waiting for work. But if the actor is fortunate enough to be working, is it necessary to spend time (and money) on so-called craft development?

Cast in a play, the actor's responsibility is to the play, to further the author's concept. All exploration is to illuminate the play, to solve the problems of the play (not the problems of the actor) and to encourage the group's collective effort. That experience naturally leads to artistic growth. But work is not always available (to put it mildly), and it is qualitatively different from the work the actor will do in a laboratory.

The work in a laboratory—the work in my laboratory—is

committed to deepening and enlarging the resources of the mature actor and to making them more accessible. It is the work of testing, discarding, and constructing chancy new pathways that will allow the actor's intuition to flourish, as well as changing old and constricting craft approaches. Stimulating personal discoveries are made in laboratory explorations that are not always possible in the paid rehearsal.

Working on one's self can also mean discovering and discarding bad habits, acquired inevitably by the need to accede to the industry's constant demands to use only the most public self. The actor needs the laboratory to integrate pieces of herself that she has never consciously put to work, has never needed before. She needs a place to explore characters for which the media and the profession think she's "wrong." She needs a place to discover how "right" she is in those parts that are "not right" for her, a place to find unexpectedly successful solutions. Even more important, perhaps, she needs a place where she can fail and "fail better" (Beckett). Fail embarrassingly, outrageously. Or to succeed, unexpectedly, in a whole new way. So clearly, this work on the self becomes work on creating a character.

There can be behavioral and psychological elements necessary for a character, the truth of which one actor will find easily, while another will stay resistant, unengaged. One actor may be easy with anger and aggression; another may not. One actor revels in sensuality and sexuality, while another, when it's demanded of him, is uncomfortable. Male actors need to explore the "female" within themselves, and women need to get comfortable with their "male" self.

Such internal roadblocks can best be addressed in a laboratory, before having to confront them when cast. Working in a long run of a play or a TV series for some years is a blessing financially, an insurance policy against another year with nothing, as well as valuable exposure in the industry; but such good luck asks the actor to use only a limited part of himself day after day. Other selves, unused, may atrophy. Additionally, the actor is told, "Just use yourself, just be present." All good advice. But the hidden irony is: "Yes, but which 'self'?" The actor spends a lifetime discovering and developing many, many selves—hidden, heroic, murderous selves.

The actor in his life laboratory and in his day-to-day work on play after play begins to recognize the need to confront and categorize these different selves. However small they may be within his psyche, the actor must be willing to offer them up in rehearsal. He needs a place to learn how to access the different selves that he is beginning to unearth, and when cast—however undeveloped they may be—extend them and be willing to reveal what had remained hidden. It is daunting. Which self, which particular "you," is asked for by the playwright or screenwriter? Which "you" will you bring to the work that day?

The actor is always changing. These many different "selves" are always in flux. The paint is no longer the same paint. Red, at forty, is not the same red as it was at age twenty-five. At fifty, injustice that once brought rage now brings sad resignation. I want my class to be a safe yet challenging place to access an actor's changing selves.

In life, we continually play different parts, sometimes consciously, sometimes not. Often our friends and family make us aware of pieces of ourselves that have emerged unconsciously, and that can shock and disturb: "Well, that's not my little girl; I just don't recognize you," or "You're acting like my father," or "Stop playing God!" We are all many selves and we play many parts, as Shakespeare reminds us. Actors take that truth and bend it into art. Making all the selves part of an actor's craft takes work. It takes courage. That is what a laboratory is for.

THE FIRST DAY

Actors who are invited into my class have completed a course of study and begun their careers. The invitation follows an interview, after which we have mutually decided that, in fact, this actor needs what I do and needs it now. He now understands that I have no secrets, no brilliant new ways, that I do not, in fact, teach acting. It is not a "how to" class.

When the work begins, I am not so foolish as to think I can be of any use to them until I have begun to understand the various elements that make up their talents, highly developed or undernourished as they may be. I begin by looking for those actor chops that are strong, fully developed, affirmed and reaffirmed by professional experience. These I leave alone. I focus on those other aspects of the actor's talent—unused, hidden, uncomfortable—that when uncovered and explored can become accessible and craftworthy. This is an important part of our work together. I am looking for the actor unmasked. When the work begins, the door to the class is shut: no visitors, no auditors. There are only the actors, who begin to depend on one another as well as on me.

On the actors' first day in class, I ask for two monologues, one contemporary, the other with heightened language, usually Shakespeare. I make sure they understand that this is not an audition, that I have already decided that they are actors with whom I want to work and that their monologues are tools for us to play with as we "learn" each other. And play is exactly what I plan for them to do. For the next forty-five minutes, we play with improvisations, transformations (physical and emotional). I have them clown, sing, dance, even skip, as well as break a text apart and put it back together. Not only will I learn more about them, but they will also begin to be welcomed and integrated into the workshop as I look to discover what the word "acting" means to them. To put into words what will inevitably be incomplete, here is what I look for to help me discover how much or how little is already available in each new actor and how much needs development.

TEMPERAMENT AND RISIBILITY

- The quickness of truthful emotional response to stimulation
- The allowing of the unexpected giggle or the sudden down-draft of emotion to arrive unmasked

PHYSICAL SENSIBILITY AND AFFECTABILITY

- A body that responds viscerally and visibly to the smallest internal thrust
- A body that is capable of expressing content without pre-thought, plan, or even language

LANGUAGE

- The physical pleasure in using consonants and vowels as weapons to achieve an end
- The ability to experience a perfect verbal way to express an idea

A SENSE OF HUMOR

- About oneself and about the world
- Recognition, acceptance, and a sharing of the fool within oneself
- Pleasure in decoding what's funny in the world, expressed verbally and physically

THE BREATH

- How expandable, how deflatable is the diaphragm
- How much does the actor live on it, speak on it, hold and expel it

I know that mostly I'm looking for the unknowables: How much of childlikeness is left in the actor? How musical is the non-musician? How danceable is the non-dancer?

AFTER THE FIRST DAY . . .

The work, week to week, is always changing, except in the broadest outline. I do not have a curriculum. There is no roadmap. My work is an improvisation, depending on the needs of a particular actor in a specific scene or exercise. The work is not generally about "making good scene," but is rather about actor growth.

The form of each class depends on how many scenes there are, how many exercises have been planned. The content of the class, however, is totally different each time. It depends entirely on the work the actors bring in on that day. I have no preconceived idea what I'm going to teach or what's going to be on my plate.

GROUP WORK, EXERCISE WORK

The day begins with the actors on their backs on the floor. They are practicing muscular relaxation, concentration, and an idiosyncratic approach to the creative state. When I think the room is concentrated, I will give them improvisations to stretch their imaginations, research their histories, and enrich their sensory capabilities. The hour belongs to the actor. She will further investigate and develop the self that she will bring to work, whether in class or in a professional rehearsal. In so doing, she will find new tools and new areas of exploration.

Next there will be individual exercises suggested by me or chosen by the actor and developed at home. These are both classic exercises, learned from my own teachers and changed (sometimes unrecognizably) by me, and also exercises of my own design—all organized to attack craft inadequacies or to discover new ways to enhance character behavior, external and internal.

These exercises, among others, focus on: a remembered place; an exploration of the dream life; and one's personal clown. Other exercises develop character using animal transformations and close inspection of the sights and sounds (some real, some imagined) of paintings. (Yes, Caravaggio and Rembrandt are great acting teachers.)

SCENE WORK

Finally, the major tool of the laboratory is prepared scene work, rehearsed privately and then rehearsed in front of the class. Sometimes the rehearsals are early ones; sometimes they are late. *But only the next rehearsal.* No audience, *therefore no performances.* The scenes are the machine that actors use in the laboratory to explore new and never-before-tried ways of putting together—one at a time—all the required elements in the work on a play: text, character, partner, place, and event. At times, scenes for the laboratory are chosen to focus on actor development, rather than to solve the problems of the play (which is required when you're cast). Never interrupted the first time they are presented, the scenes are often repeated, reorganized, and brought back to class two or three times.

Scene work depends on the actor's effort to be clear about what specific element or elements he wants to explore in this day's work. Rather than trying to solve everything in every rehearsal, I encourage actors to make choices. Today's rehearsal may need a more detailed exploration of logical character behavior. So it may be that in today's work, other elements (such as the strong action of the character or the full attention to the partner) may be under-expressed. An actor may also choose to explore some personal obstacle that needs confronting, or some way of using himself that needs room to flourish and which the play gives him an opportunity to strengthen. Rehearsing for that element may leave others unattended. That is as it should be in a rehearsal. One useful choice is to rehearse making no choices, knowing nothing, rehearsing only to find out what the scene is about. It takes practice to rehearse without preconceived decisions, to allow the text to lead, to live totally with the other actors.

On another day, one actor will test herself with Shakespeare, a writer she has not yet explored professionally. Do it well, do it badly, taste the iambic. Another actor needs to understand the concept of an action and storytelling. Yet another actor might usefully practice being absolutely present in every moment, without concern for what is correct/incorrect, right/wrong, good/bad—or for what in later rehearsals must be accomplished to meet the demands of the play. When researching a specific character, exploring counterintuitive or exaggerated choices, physical and internal, may reveal the landscape of the play. The opportunities for valuable discoveries in scene work are without end.

After exercise work and scene work, actors are encouraged to comment on the work of their colleagues, but within specific parameters: positive changes that they see from past work; the specific work to which the actor was committed today; basic elements such as relaxation and concentration. Criticism after the scene should be directed at what the actor chose to work on. Directorial comments are to be avoided. If an actor likes another's work or thinks it was lacking, he is expected to ask of himself: "Why? What was done or not done that made me respond?" We are not an audience; we are colleagues.

PRIVATE IN PUBLIC AND THE CLASS COMMUNITY

Beyond tools and tasks, beyond ways old and new, what is most important, most necessary, and most difficult is that the actor practice allowing his private self to become public—in both the simplest and most complicated ways. Only then can unused elements of a talent be brought more creatively to the workplace. In the laboratory, practicing being completely private in front of many people strengthens the actor's recognition and understanding of its value when he performs. Exploring and experiencing what it means to be "private in public" *is* difficult. It is hard enough to be private in private, difficult to confront yourself, to be completely present without attitude.Being yourself alone in public is what you must offer.

Once the class begins to see change in an actor's work, something important happens to the class as a whole. Success for one becomes success for everyone. A community emerges. These researchers, these actors, are now listening to each other. They stop judging and offer help. A good professional acting class should strengthen and develop greater trust and reliance among actors, a positive experience that the actor will bring to her professional life.

Chapter 17
What Makes a Good Teacher?

What makes a good teacher? For that matter, what makes a good teacher of acting?

PASSION
Passion about the subject. Passion about sharing it. Passion about the beauty and elegance of a solved problem—of the person or of the page—whether it's the math student's neat clarification or the actor suddenly discovering an elusive, previously hidden truth. Passion about craft.

THE NURTURING INSTINCT
Deep, personal gratification at the growth and development of the student. The willingness to be an instrument in the fulfillment of another's success.

CURIOSITY
This seems a small thing but is in fact large. It means an easily excited, open-ended open-mindedness about the new, the pleasure

in a student seeing something that you missed—and therefore the willingness to be wrong. It means learning from those being taught.

It is not possible to always teach at the top of one's game. But we aim for it. And when we reach it for an hour we should celebrate. And when we lose it, and don't know how or why, we weep.

Chapter 18
Out on a Limb

If an actor were to look back at the end of life and examine her work with objectivity, and if she put all considered successes in one basket and all the failures in another, the failure basket would be by far the heavier. The more mature, original, and even brilliant the artist, the fuller the "F" basket. In both are actor choices that can be life changers, as well as those that are forgettable. The fully realized successes want us to look at them every so often, and we do. They encourage us, remind us of our worth. But the failures—large or small—return unbidden and bring us hurt, anxiety, doubt.

Failures are remembered by others when we want nothing more than to close the book. I am not discussing the failure of an actor to earn a living, to get hired, to solve the puzzle of the commercial theater. Too often those are failures of the theater itself. Of course the actor must take responsibility for learning the business of acting and making a career. Nevertheless, our industry allows some of the most talented, accomplished, and exciting actors to give up after they have confronted years of rejection. But I am not concerned with those failures here. I am discussing the actor's craftwork—the wrong answers, foolish choices, unnoticed opportunities.

Are failures always inevitable in the work process? Yes. Are they necessary? Are they useful? Absolutely. For the performing artist, failure means the inability, the unsuccessful but continuing effort, to get that laugh, to find the right physical expression, the deepest inner connection, the truth in a relationship. We reject the almost right. We keep trying and keep failing. Until, sometimes, a eureka moment. The road to fulfillment of an aesthetic idea is paved with failures.

True, it is the fear of failure, not failure itself, which is the enemy. In a larger sense, the artist must hold to her commitment to a theatrically unusual, startling, productive idea, even if it is greeted by naysayers as inadequate or unacceptable. The artist herself will discover if that idea is a dismal failure or, in spite of the naysayers, a great beginning. Chance it. It is that fear of failure that makes the artist settle for what's easy, conventional, acceptable. To be willing to fail, to have your eye on a truth that is perhaps hidden and elusive, and to pursue it close to ridicule, even to derision, takes extraordinary courage. Actor courage.

This observation is not some philosophical riff. It's about the work—actor-work, rehearsal-work, and performance-work. The actor must be willing to make choices that may fail, go too far, exaggerate, look foolish. To fail again and again has buried in it the potential for developing that one illuminating and deeply satisfying moment that is the secret of good acting, important acting. When we work, what we want is just one moment of truth. Then another moment, and then another.

These moments can be small or large, small moments that are about handling an object and large moments that last for pages and turn a play around. It is like stringing together jewels into a necklace. Theater artists are not easily satisfied. We throw away and then reclaim. We know when we are not present, when we haven't found what we are looking for. We know when we are lying, even when our coworkers don't. We search for each moment fully concentrated. That necklace is what we are after.

Of course, it hardly ever happens that way. Every performance has in it moments of the middle ground, the OK, the not very satisfying. It's not a place where the actor wants to remain. Then there are the failures (always). Those perfect moments found yesterday but inexplicably lost today. Looking for yesterday's truth, you founder. Never mind. Live only on today's truth. Sometimes you will have to lie. Lie well. Know you are lying. Just do not ever lie to yourself. The audience will see only the necklace—it's quite lovely—with all its flaws.

If you have lost a highly charged emotional moment, fully do the rehearsed physical behavior that comes from a strong, internal need. Even if tonight your internal motor won't turn over, tonight do only the physical action. Do not act the emotional need. Do not lie the emotion—even when the other character says: "Why are you angry?" Do not lie anger. But do threaten, until you see the actor turn pale, as he always has before. Pluck the beard, dance the war dance. In other words, do fully what you always do, and do it even better. Just don't try to be anything, including angry. I remind the actor: feelings are the result of an action. Feelings, if they are not inserted, not watched for, erupt on their own, unasked and powerful.

One more thing about being wrong, about spending the day,

the week, opening clams, thinking they are oysters, and looking for pearls. The magnificent fuck-up is a world every actor, every artist, every scientist inhabits. Being wrong in the scientist's lab or in the theater rehearsal hall is to be expected, welcomed, though there are major differences between the two. Not recognizing an error by a scientist developing a new medicine, or an architect designing a bridge, can kill. That's their reality, their truth. The actor has a different reality. It's a non-truth but a psychological reality. It concerns death, in this case the death of the actor. Yes, we make jokes, but without really joking: "I died out there," "He's getting killed," "It's like a funeral." Or conversely, "I killed them." Life and death. In our work, the possibility of hurt, of psychological wounds, feels real. It takes courage, night after night. Why should it matter so? It's just a job, we tell ourselves. But it does matter.

It matters because painters, scientists, architects, writers all get to sign off on their finished work in silence, in the privacy of their studio. Good, bad, brilliantly evolved or dismally unrealized, their art is done. The writer can hit "delete," the painter can paint over, the movie director edits in a studio. But the actor? After the last run-through, after the last dress rehearsal when the "ghost light" is figuratively turned off, with the house lights out and the stage lights up, the actor waits in the dark, adrenaline pumping, breath short, waiting to step out in front of a thousand strangers, and make art. All the revealing, all the truth telling, the chance taking, the painful slippery struggles, must be dared in front of them. For the actor-artist, the moment of creation happens in public, where he is most vulnerable, where he stands naked at the moment of creation. It is a brave thing to do. It is also fulfilling and enriching to be unmasked, revealed behind the thin curtain of the character.

If you've been terribly wrong, you'll discover it. As a wound to the heart, you'll know it. We care, deeply and more than we are sometimes willing to admit, about how much we can affect them, change them. We care that they "get us"—that they are enlivened, brought to their knees weeping, or lifted out of their seats laughing. So when they don't get us (and we know when they don't), it hurts. It is a little like dying.

Chapter 19
Obstacles

The obstacles—roadblocks, really—that have always stood in the way of an actor pursuing a rewarding, successful career can be separated into two categories: those that come from the actor and those that come from the profession. First, the business. Among the most damnable and paradoxical in the industry is that they won't hire you without a track record, and you can't have a track record if they won't hire you. An actor needs an agent and must have contact with casting directors, and they won't even consider him until they have seen him work. Well, the theater world is as it is: unresponsive, relentlessly rejecting, and driven by luck.

There are many more professional obstacles, too many to list, and they change from one generation to the next. Swimming upstream has never been easy. In the first half of the twentieth century, all actors' names that were not Aryan sounding had to be changed. Foreign-sounding or Jewish-sounding names were forbidden. The size of the nose, particularly for women, was a serious issue. Plastic surgeons specializing in rhinoplasty made fortunes. We should all be grateful to Gina Lollobrigida and Barbra Streisand, who stood by their names and noses, respectively. There have been many other positive changes in casting over the years, but actors from ethnic minorities still confront difficulty becoming part of the American acting community.

Then there is typecasting. Agents and managers will tell you to get to know what type you are, to learn how the industry sees you. I understand that deadening logic. If you are lucky and begin to work, you will live by being categorized: "You are this type, not that type. Sorry." The best of us refuse to let the industry do it and we try to find ways to get around it. In 1943, Lois Wheeler, then a classmate of mine, who was a recent graduate of the Neighborhood Playhouse, decided to audition for the part of Margaret, a twelve-year-old girl, in Paul Osborn's *The Innocent Voyage*. The play was produced by the Theatre Guild, the biggest producers at the time. Lois was already a full-figured, beautiful woman in her twenties. To recreate herself as a twelve-year-old, she removed her makeup, flattened her chest, wore flat shoes, and arranged to have her younger sister pretend to be her guardian to take her to the audition. Laurence Langner and Theresa Heilbrun, big-time producers, were amazed at the maturity of this "child" they saw before them. She got the part and opened on Broadway to excellent reviews. She continued her masquerade with some difficulty, even after the show opened. But Lois was a heavy smoker, and at lunchtime she would sneak off to grab a cigarette in a coffee shop as far from the theater as possible. One day, the stage manager came to eat lunch in the same diner, and that ended her ruse. The play's publicists were delighted, and the story ran in all the New York newspapers.

THE DEADENING EFFECT OF CATEGORIZING

In 1942 Actor's Equity started the *Players Guide*, in which all member actors (whether new to the profession or with twenty years on

Broadway) listed themselves with a picture and bio. There were categories: "Leading Man or Woman," "Juvenile," or "Character-Comedian." Directors and producers used the guide. We hoped they would turn the page and find us. In 1951, I listed myself under the heading "Character-Comedian," among the old guys. That was as close as I could get to how the industry saw me, and even cast me.

This categorizing came from the nineteenth century and earlier, when even contracts had categories, such as "Second Business" for actors who always played the friend of the leading man. I was told by one agent (Chamberlain Brown, who made his bones early in the twentieth century) that I could never be cast as a soldier. "Not the type," he said. (I wish he had told that to my draft board.)[8]

Much of the worst of mechanistic casting—once the professional norm—is over, although inevitably there will always be typecasting. In television and film, particularly, the concern in casting is for the actor, as he walks in, to look and sound exactly like what's written. It is understandable, given hurry-up television and the camera close-up. But it has infected the live theater and actor training as well. There are now classes that teach how the entertainment world sees you—how to learn your type. Perhaps that must be done to get work. Perhaps not. If the actor investigates the private, the very dark or the very bright, what he brings to the audition will be enriched, surprising.

---

8. Other colorful designations that date back to the 1800s include: "1st Light Comedian," "1st Singing Man," "Heavy Man," "Walking Gentleman," and finally "Utility." V. C. Clinton-Baddeley, *It'll Be All Right on the Night* (London: Putnam, 1954), 114.

What is lost in this categorizing is the actor's deep satisfaction and the audience's pleasure in the miracle of total transformation, character to character, physical, emotional, and, finally, visual.

In the first half of the twentieth century and through the 1960s, actors were still being taught theatrical makeup—they had to have makeup kits with crepe (fake) hair, spirit gum to attach it, nose putty, and, yes, grease paint. And cold cream—tons of it. Even more important than their external look, actors were expected to create characters internally and to reveal a transformed, private, unrecognizable "self" that illuminated the character and enriched the play. You were expected to play old, young, thin, fat, and that you would be able to play other than your public self. Unfortunately, today it is seldom that an actor is asked for much more than variations of the self she brings into the casting office.

The commercial world in which actors must work tends to see the actor the same as any product in need of marketing: "How can we reach the largest number of buyers?" Not with the product's essential goodness, but with its look. The toothpaste is good, but it needs to have a new box, new colors. Actors are not commodities, not products. Push back. Actors are not fools. How we look, how we are received by audiences, is important. So bend, perhaps. But do not let them bend you out of shape into something you are not and don't want to be.

AN EVEN GREATER OBSTACLE

Even when professional barriers are breached, there always remain personal obstacles. I once asked a well-known actor what he would identify as the strongest obstacle to furthering his career. The answer, after a moment, was one word: "Me." The honesty of that answer is one that all artists confront. There are seemingly endless aspects of "me" that the actor, whose instrument is his whole self, must work to overcome: vanishing self-confidence, apathy, arrogance, timidity, unwillingness to change. Worst is the mask, the public face that the actor must learn how to drop.

The "me" problems endure for an actor's entire career. There is a bedeviling paradox: The most experienced, the most accomplished, and even the most talented actors suffer the most doubts and painful insecurities, while the least experienced and least knowledgeable experience the fewest fears—filled with certainty, their egos have the fewest vulnerabilities. The mature artist discovers that the more she works, the more she sees what's missing, the more she senses deeper truths that have yet to be accomplished, the more she realizes her own inadequacies. Yet it is exactly these awful insecurities, devastating doubts, and wounds that refuse to heal that the actor wrestles into art.

SOLUTIONS

Putting aside the age-old problem of the artist confronting himself, the barricades the professional theater throws up can seem insurmountable. More and more, actors do not wait for show business to find them. They are joining with think-alike actors to create their own theater in basements and in attics, in storefronts and in parking lots, and joining with think-alike directors and, if they are lucky, promising writers whose work is stimulating, challenging, and with which they can grow. I'm not talking about showcases, those one-time, thrown-together heartbreakers attended reluctantly by one or two interns from an agent's office. In the last sixty years (at least), some of the most important writers, directors, and actors made the world pay attention in small, out-of-the-way venues. In New York, Broadway is still capable of supporting serious writers, but increasingly it is becoming a spectacle theater. Even off-Broadway is a million-dollar business now. Off-off and way-off-Broadway is and has been for years the incubator for actors as well as writers. Chicago, Louisville, Seattle, Baltimore, and many other cities also host "startup" companies in which serious young theater artists develop interesting work.

In describing what it is to live as an actor in the American theater, I've left out foolish plays, unresponsive colleagues, sadistic directors, no money, and empty theaters. I leave them out because every art worth fighting for has obstacles. Overcoming them makes success even tastier. And in the struggle to overcome, some success (even a small success) and some affirmation are necessary. Otherwise it's hard to tell if this is the life in which you belong. But if you don't need acting, if acting isn't your best "high," if you really are at peace without it, then you should find something else about which you are passionate.

One important final point: be ready. If you get lucky (because sometimes that's what it is) and are offered a great part, a career changer, be ready. Be ready to use everything your talent can offer the play. Dustin Hoffman, a rather small and not particularly imposing young man, and at the time without much of a track record, was offered a great part in a new off-Broadway play called *Journey of the Fifth Horse*. He was ready. I saw it. He hit a home run. Geraldine Page was once offered an off-Broadway redo of a failed Tennessee Williams play: *Summer and Smoke*. She was ready.

"Yes," you may say, "but what exactly does it mean to be ready?" First, it means keeping exactly that question in front of you.

The question is what is important. Ask yourself what now in your work needs attention. You already enjoy the strengths, but what are your weaknesses? Examine the question of readiness in terms of your external technique as well as the internal. You must get to know your instrument as well as Vladimir Horowitz, the famous concert pianist, knew all aspects of his particular piano, which accompanied him wherever he performed. He also understood his hands, their specific muscularity. The more the artist understands and respects his external instrument, the more he can access his internal genius, his "musicality." How else to be ready? Make room for your clown, your fool, as well as your dark, forbidden side. And also your hero.

In the professional theater, the number of actors who were offered really good parts (with great potential) who were finally, well, just "adequate" is beyond counting. There are thousands of good actors in New York and in many other great cities. Adequate is simply not good enough.

My ruminations on what helps-hurts, what starts-stops the expansion of a committed actor's potential is contained in one repeated idea: Actors must act. And act. And act. Find a group. Find a place. Don't be too choosy. Take good parts or bad. Actors need an audience.

Then there are the moments, not too often, when we know that we have done it to our fullest capability, no matter what others may think. Then we know why we will keep on doing it, why we choose to make a life of it. We may wish we didn't care so viscerally. But without that deep caring, we can never have that moment where we sit quietly, fulfilled. As Hamlet promises us: "If it be not now, yet it will come. The readiness is all" (Act V, Scene 2).

Epilogue

MEMOIRS: HITS, MISSES, AND SMALL CATASTROPHES

As the war in Europe ended—on May 9, 1945, "VE" (Victory in Europe) Day—millions of GIs exhaled. My company of the 101st Airborne was bivouacked in central France, where I had recently returned after a hospital stay in Dijon, thanks to a nasty case of trench foot.

Every American soldier in Europe had a number based on their months served in the Army, a higher number for months overseas, and a still higher number if he'd seen combat. Soldiers were discharged based on this number. What we dreaded was being sent to fight in the war against Japan. I had a decently high number, so I knew that I was soon to be on my way home and to my life in the theater.

Some weeks later, I read in *Stars and Stripes*, the Army newspaper, that performers—actors—were wanted to produce entertainment for the troops cooling their heels and waiting to be sent east or west to home. The article listed an address in Paris. I had a grand idea. Because all now was a little lax, I would get an afternoon pass, stretch it into a weekend (sometimes called AWOL), and hitchhike to join my friend and acting buddy Dolph in the 17th Airborne (which was closer to Paris). Off we would go to offer ourselves to Special Services. I found Dolph in the Headquarters Company. We and another actor friend he'd met in the army hitchhiked to Paris with the help of two army trucks, a horse-drawn hay cart, and an ambulance.

When we arrived in the still-dark morning, we went to the Red Cross, cleaned up, and slept for an hour and a half. We walked outside into the mists of Paris on a spring morning. All Dolph and I knew about France at peace was from the excellent French movies we had seen, starring all those great actors: Jean-Louis Barrault, Jean Gabin, Danielle Darieux, Louis Jouvet.

At Special Services, we were greeted by a corporal, an older man, small. Unbelievably, it was a name we all knew: Corp. Louis Sher. He was the biggest agent in Hollywood—he was Bob Hope's agent. He couldn't have been nicer. He came out of the captain's office and announced, "Captain Logan will see you now." We were ushered into the office and we met the captain. It was Joshua Logan. The Joshua Logan. The director Logan of the biggest and the best of what was on Broadway.

We sat there, stunned, as he chatted us up, interested in our war (rather different from his). When he heard that we had studied with Sanford Meisner at the Neighborhood Playhouse, he asked: "How is that son of a bitch?" (I have no memory of our answer.) After a few minutes he clapped us on the back and said, "Absolutely, guys, we'll recruit you. We need guys like you." We floated out of the office into Paris in the spring.

This needed some very special celebration. The nearest cafe would not do. From those French movies, we knew about the Hotel George Cinq and its restaurant. It was the Waldorf, the Plaza, the

Carlyle of Paris. Off we went. We three privates, giddy in our paratrooper uniforms, white scarves, white laces in our boots, were greeted by the *maître d'*. In my high school French I began to explain we were celebrating a personal triumph. He interrupted, and with perfect English welcomed us into a huge, gorgeous room. He took us to a table and helped us order the wine and food. For the next hour and a half we proceeded to get ecstatically drunk.

Halfway through this delirium, Marlene Dietrich arrived on the arm of—really—Jean Gabin! (Gabin and Dietrich—the Bogart and Bacall of their time.) Dietrich was the poster girl of the army overseas, and she always dressed in a paratrooper uniform, the 101st Airborne, my outfit. There she was, parachute wings pinned to her lapel, and on her arm the patch of the 101st. And there we were, three privates getting higher and higher.

The bill came, and Paris in the spring became winter. We had not nearly enough. With great urging and much laughter, the damnable majority of two decided that I would be the one to ask Dietrich for help. They dared me to do it. I accepted the challenge. I got to my feet and began to weave my way past tables.

Halfway there, Gabin and Dietrich saw me coming. Gabin had his elbows on the table and his head in his hands. He didn't move. Dietrich smiled. What a smile. I arrived at the table, breathless, and began to, tried to, explain. But her hand was already in her purse, and as I was mumbling, leaning on her table, steadying myself, she slipped something into my right hand. Gabin looked up but still did not move. I backed away, as one does from a queen, and returned to our table, aware that the dining room was watching and smiling. I sat down and looked at what was in my hand. It was more than enough.

I received much drunken approbation from my friends. There was still some wine, and we raised our glasses and toasted "La Dietrich" from across the room. She smiled and lifted a glass. Later, as Gabin and Dietrich got up to leave, the waiter brought me a note, written in eyebrow pencil, on a torn piece of menu: "Is it enough? Because there's more . . . D." I made a gesture of "No, no, we're fine," and out they went.

After Paris, my friends went back to the 17th Airborne, and I went back to the 101st. We all expected to hear from Captain Logan at any moment and to be in rehearsal once again. But we never heard another word from Special Services. That may have been because two weeks after I got back, my company was transferred to the 82nd Airborne and sent to Berlin to serve as Occupation Troops in the American Zone (Berlin had been divided into zones: American, English, French, and Russian).

Soon after I arrived in Berlin and bivouacked in extraordinarily comfortable (for the American Army, anyway) former SS barracks, someone from the American Forces Network radio station, which broadcast throughout Europe, must have searched through Army records and found that I had a background in theater and asked me to join the AFN Berlin staff. "No thanks," I said. I was with my friends, I was in an exciting new environment, and I knew I would be on my way home within six months. The program director said, "Fine, but come to lunch with us anyway." They sent a car for me—me, a private. I entered a mansion (it had originally belonged to Max Schmeling, the world-famous German boxer). The dining room was furnished with linen and silver. Astonished, I sat, took out a cigarette, and was about to light it, but the waiter was already there with a lighter. That did it. I joined the American Forces Network Berlin. I emceed five terrific GI jazz musicians—"Jive at Five," it was called—and I became a nighttime disc jockey.

Early in the Allied Occupation of Berlin, there had been a strict army nonfraternization policy: GIs could not fraternize with German women (or men, for that matter). But at one point the Army relented and asked some German church leaders to choose carefully some young ladies to bring to the opening of a brand-new social club. Because ending the nonfraternization policy was an important event, the AFN Berlin's program director decided we should do a radio remote there with a live audience.

When I heard that Dietrich was in Berlin visiting her mother, I had a big idea: ask her to come to the opening, where I could pay her back the money she had given to me in Paris. I sent her a message, reminding her. She contacted my commanding officer and said she'd be delighted.

My cohost and I wrote a script with a running joke. We told nobody that Dietrich would be there. It began with the MC questioning me about my acting life in New York. He asked if I knew any famous people. I said, "Yes, a few," and I listed a few, Marlene Dietrich among them. He said, "No, you don't know her." I said, "Yes! Really, I do." "I don't believe you," he said. "You don't?" and then I called, "Marlene, will you come out here, please?" She did and gave me a big hug. I reminded her of the money I had borrowed in Paris and paid her back. Another hug, and it was over.

I was asked to stay on in Berlin as a civilian contractor, even though I had earned enough points to go home. Stay in Berlin? Now, when I could be back with the whole New York theater waiting to embrace me?! A few months later, at the end of 1945, I was home, ready to act.

Soon after I got back, I began to work both in the new medium of ·

commercial television and in summer stock. My first stock company job was in 1947 in Olney, Maryland, where I got my Equity Card. The contract was written to "Bob Howard"—my real name. Equity told me, "Sorry, we already have a Bob Howard. Choose another name." Misery. And after three months of searching baby books with my wife, Betty, I chose "Michael." (In the radio soap opera *Helen Trent*, the leading lady had a poet/lover named "Mmmmiiiiichael." At fifteen, the sound of it sent my hormones racing; I haven't heard it said that way since.) But I've been Michael for the last sixty-nine years.

At that company in Olney, the director Charles Dubin, along with my good friends James Karen, Ruth White, and others, went to the producers and told them we wouldn't work in a segregated theater. (The great National Theatre in Washington, DC, was still segregated, although many actors had tried unsuccessfully to deseg-regate it.) To her credit, the producer, Evelyn Freyman, an executive with AFRA (the American Federation of Radio Artists), was abso-lutely willing as long as we didn't make a big deal of it and simply sat everyone, white and black, wherever they had paid to sit.

During that season the company received a letter from a Professor Frank M. Snowden Jr., chairman of the Classics Department at Howard University:

> Gentlemen, my wife and I recently had the pleasure of seeing a performance of *The Vinegar Tree* at the Olney Theatre. We are negroes. With the deepest sincerity, I wish to express my congratulations for your courage in permit-ting the negroes in this community to enjoy with others your dramatic offerings . . . Your courage and your spirit bring to my mind a passage in Thomas Wolfe's *You Can't*

Go Home Again: "I think the true discovery of America is before us. I think the true fulfillment of our spirit, of our people, of our mighty and immortal land is yet to come. . ." Like Wolfe, I believe that the true discovery of America is before us. However, the fulfillment of our spirit, of our people, will be possible only when more Americans become imbued with a spirit such as yours.

A victory. Actors can make a difference.

My small career was starting. From the very beginnings in 1940, when I was cast as Snorky, a one-armed Civil War veteran in Augustine Daily's *Under the Gaslight*, which toured Vermont Grange halls, I was always cast in extreme character parts, at which I became very proficient. I was hardly ever cast just as a "young man."

Another company I worked in was in Laconia, New Hampshire. It was directed by Peter Kass, a friend of Clifford Odets. In 1949 Odets had just finished his latest play, *The Country Girl*, and was anxious to see it on its feet. He asked Peter to schedule a tryout of this new play in New Hampshire. Peter cast me as the doctor who came to see Georgie, the leading lady, with the bad news that she had cancer.

During the day, the company rehearsed *The Country Girl*, and at night we played E.Y. ("Yip") Harburg's *Finian's Rainbow*. I played Finian (always character parts), and a young Cliff Robertson played the Leprechaun. Rehearsals of *The Country Girl* went well. I was experiencing a new work from a major American playwright and helping bring it to life!

After the first performance, the actor playing the lead role lost his voice—totally. Odets was upset, wanting to get a sense of his play on its feet, and facing the possibility of a wasted week or two, asked me if I could get up in it quickly—even if I held the book or needed prompting. Actors understand that these extraordinary requests— "Be a hero! Save the day!"—are not to be refused.

That meant no performance Tuesday night, no performance Wednesday matinee, and then I would play it Wednesday night and for the rest of the run. It meant thirty-six hours of no sleep, memorizing the words. More important: the internal journey as well as the physical track, the entrances and exits. On Wednesday, the second opening of *The Country Girl*, with me playing Frank Elgin, a very large part, went as well as one could hope. Presumably, Clifford received some value from this turn of events. He and the audience were very generous to me.

Parenthetically, because I played the lead, there couldn't be a doctor and therefore there was no cancer for Georgie—nor was there ever again. Clifford realized it wasn't necessary.

Back in New York, as the play was being readied for Broadway, produced by Dwight Deere Wiman, Odets was kind enough—or was it gratitude?—to offer me the part of the young and untried author who writes the play within the play. He told me the money in the budget for this character was $150 a week, at a time when the Equity minimum was $100.

I went in to negotiate—why didn't I get an agent? Foolish, foolish, Michael!—with the general manager, Forrest Haring, considered to be the toughest, meanest managing director on Broadway. He was surprisingly friendly and chatty. Then he offered me a contract at $100 a week. I knew he had in front of him a budget that marked the part at a hundred and half. "No," I said, "I won't do it for minimum." He smirked. "Sorry, kid, that's what it's marked as."

"I can't," I said.

"Sorry," he said and went on with his work.

Confused, I got up and walked to the door. As I opened it, the demon emerged from behind Haring's nice-guy mask. He was nasty, angry at losing. "All right, sit down! A hundred and a half!" A victory!

We rehearsed on the stage of the magnificent Lyceum Theatre, where the play would open. Clifford himself was directing, with Lee Strasberg, by then my teacher and Odets's mentor and friend, sitting in the back of the theater as a kind of gray eminence to help Clifford.

The first week of rehearsal seemed uneventful with the brilliant actors Uta Hagen and Steven Hill and the movie star Paul Kelly, the leads, having many private conversations with Clifford and the rest of us doing our work. I was aware of a rather brusque, dismissive attitude from Dwight Wiman, which I thought was because of my fifty-dollar victory. Anyway, I had friends in high places.

My part, Paul Unger, was an interesting challenge. Written as somewhat bland and somewhat opaque—as often happens when writers write writers like themselves—it wanted only me, uncovered, present, available, responsive, involved in an exciting adventure. It was a new acting experience for me, a part wanting no external or even internal characterization. Simply me and the situation. Other than Wiman, it seemed to be going well. Clifford's notes were few and positive. Mr. Strasberg's only comment ever was "fine, fine."

After rehearsal on the twelfth day, Clifford asked to talk to me. Rather than talking up on the stage or in seats in the house, he took me to a stairwell, up-center, behind the back wall of the Lyceum. "Michael," he said, "Wiman thinks you look too Jewish. He's a bit of an anti-Semite. Ignore him. I want you, that's what matters. You're doing fine." Then he left, I think not wanting to be seen having a private conversation with me. I sat there on the steps, stunned. I was aware he had given me a secret. It was something I had to keep to myself. I sat there for many minutes. I was Jewish-proud, but not Jewish-conscious. Until that moment I had never encountered in the theater what is now called being "too ethnic."

Now the farce began. The nose, I told myself, it must be the nose. Have you ever tried to see yourself in profile? It's difficult. The trained actor part of me said, "Cut it out, forget it. Play the action, get concentrated on the other actors." But that despicable little worm of self-concern, of self-watching, began to unconcentrate me, began to do Wiman's work. The part wants a young writer, watching, listening, thrilled to be part of the birth of his first play. He's passive, but present. I gave Clifford no ammunition, no strong visible presence. I should have used the anger that flooded me to inform my character, encouraging it to get more hotly involved. I should have played each action with more vigor, more completeness.

The company went to Boston for a pre-Broadway run, and I could feel the part slipping away. You can't play a negative. Eyes became averted. I think everyone knew, except me. Then I saw a friend from the Actors Studio, Joe Sullivan, a lovely, six-foot-one Irish boy scout (and a fine actor) in the audience. Then, even I knew. I was canned.

Being fired is no big deal and it happens all the time. Sometimes it's the fault of the actor, but more often it is an admission that the director and the producer made a serious error. (As a director, I had to fire an actor because his voice, as we rehearsed, sounded just like the voice of the lead actor; it was hard to tell which actor was speaking. It was my problem, but the actor paid the price.) Looking back,

I can see the producer's point of view in *The Country Girl*. I think Clifford finally saw it as well. Anti-Semitism aside, the production would not have wanted an audience to think of a young Odets as the writer in the play and therefore begin to see the play biographically. Casting Joe Sullivan put up a wall.

Postscript: the stage manager was playing the small part of the dresser in the play within a play, a money-saver for the producer. Clifford, perhaps out of guilt or shared pain, made Wiman, the producer, offer me the part. Everything in me wanted to tell him to "shove it." My first child, Christopher, was not yet a year old. I accepted and played it until it closed.

There are clear-eyed and experienced actors who would tell me "You shoulda, you coulda." Of course—me too. But I was neither in 1950. The world turns. I've learned. I never again have let one job be so terribly important.

I share the following because it concerns a man of great theater renown (and deservedly so), a man of talent, integrity, and a healthy respect for the goodness of mankind: E.Y. "Yip" Harburg, a brilliant lyricist and one of the masters of the American musical theater. In 1957, having acted in *Finian's Rainbow*—his most famous musical—and having loved the musical, I managed to direct it two times.

I had directed it the first time at the Woodstock Playhouse in upstate New York and was anxious to do it again with a full rehearsal schedule, so I jumped at the chance to direct it in New York City for the Equity Library Theatre, which then was performing at the Master's Institute on 103rd Street and Broadway. (The Equity Library Theatre was a theater financed by the union to give actors the chance to work in previously produced plays.) Harburg came to see it and was very complimentary. He wanted to talk and had some serious questions about my casting, which he explained to me over a drink after seeing the show. We talked for an hour. We talked about theater and its potential for remedying injustice.

Later that year, Harburg called me. He was in Philadelphia with the out-of-town tryout of his new musical, *Jamaica*. Yip felt he had written a truthful account of the people of the Caribbean, a "folk opera" with many satirical and political overtones. I think he thought of it as his response to *Porgy and Bess*. He hated what was happening on the stage in Philadelphia. He had written it for Harry Belafonte, who felt, together with Yip, that Caribbean culture had been violated by the resort industry. Mr. Belafonte left the show during rehearsals, citing "sickness." That wonderful talent, Lena Horne, was hired. Jack Cole came from Hollywood to do the jazzy calypso dances. David Merrick was producing, and Bobby Lewis, another big talent, was having a grand time directing. But little by little and then a lot by a lot, Yip said, it was getting away from what he had envisioned. He was miserable, angry. Would I come to Philly, telling no one, and look at it to see if anything could be done?

Apparently he was not ready to use his writer's influence because he had agreed step by step to so many of the decisions thus far. It is a dilemma confronting many important writers of the theater: the artist's desire for integrity and artistic truth running smack into the cement wall of potential Broadway success. And here Yip had David Merrick, a big-time commercial producer, as well as Robert Lewis and Lena Horne to contend with. So I agreed to have a look.

"Tell no one," he said, "I'm at the Hotel Biltmore. There'll be a ticket in your name." What I saw that night was a nightclub act with African Americans—"negroes," in those days—surrounding Ms.

Horne with Hollywood-type choreography. Gorgeous costumes, glitter, a nightclub act. After the performance, I joined Yip in his hotel room. Clearly, there was absolutely nothing to be done. It was hard for me to know what Harburg thought that he had with *Jamaica* and how he had let it come, small step by small step, to this. His hotel room was dreary: half-eaten food, unmade bed. I saw how hurt and unhappy he was. We sat, not talking much. There seemed to be nothing I could say. He knew, more than I ever could, how those little "giving in," acquiescing, steps along the way to commercial success had torpedoed his vision.

When *Jamaica* got to Broadway, the reviews were mixed, but the show ran for more than five hundred performances. Star power. Lena Horne was wonderful as usual and did what was asked of her. That splendid artist E.Y. Harburg, who was later blacklisted in Hollywood, supported his family for more than a year from the proceeds. Sometimes even hits are really misses.

THE GIFT

I have used the term "a gift" in many ways: the gift from the actor of a great laugh or of an emotional catharsis; the gift to the actor of an inspiring idea and the clarifying language that carries it; a full house is a gift, if I've not already called it so. But the most necessary, the most deeply desired gift that we actors of the theater hope we have been given in abundance is the gift of talent.

What is it? How to describe it? What is it made of? Books have been and will continue to be written about it. Certainly, it includes a deeply sentient nature, quick to respond to stimulus, a rich imagination, a love of language, an original mind, and courage enough to stand psychically naked before strangers and enjoy it. The gift of talent, large or small, must be nurtured, developed, respected, and protected. Most of all, if it is not to wither, it must be put to work. I wish you work. I wish you the soul-satisfying kick of good colleagues, a good play, a full house, and a paycheck.

Break a leg.

Acknowledgments

Acknowledgments, for the general reader, are usually a great bore. I think most people who know the writer, for better or worse, simply skip through looking for their name. Maybe every writer thinks: "Yes, but my acknowledgments are more important, my acknowledgments are serious and should interest everyone." As a matter of fact, it is what I think, too.

That's because every single name I'm about to list, every single one of these extraordinary people, is a member of the acting community, up there, onstage when the lights come up, every one trying to make a life in the theater, and yet they still made time to edit me, to affirm me, to push me into this book. Every one has been essential to my ability to put my thinkings into print. I am so very grateful to these friends, these colleagues, these fellow journeymen. And of course, to my publisher, Tad Crawford, and my editor Kelsie Besaw.

First, and most important, is my literary agent, Joseph Spieler—agent, yes, but also editor, and, most important, committed and demanding friend. Joe wanted to know everything, wanted to partake, wanted to explore and understand all that I was writing. Joe, the midwife. Hundreds of hours—years, really—did he push, complain, and stroke. And during that time, Joe has become, with a little help from me, an exciting actor. Every writer needs a Joe in his life. The most valuable thing he did, perhaps, is to help me sound like me.

Two and a half years ago, Joe brought on board Jesse Liebman, a fine actor and a member of my acting laboratory, to help me grab hold of my jumping-jack improvisational ideas—ideas that too often caused me literary whiplash. A writer himself, Jesse provided me with his exceptional organizational mind, taste that I could count on, and a willingness to do what I wanted most: to make sure that every idea, every chapter, said what I wanted it to say. The collaborative nature of our work together continues to give me pleasure.

At the beginning of this journey, there was the question of a proposal for potential publishers. For months, Rebecca Blumhagen sat with me as I struggled to do a *précis* of my life's work in fifty pages. Patient she was, and encouraging. Thank you, Rebecca.

Elyse Knight, Jenny Neale Baldwin, and later Naama Potok, went past the proposal and began to organize scattered bits and pieces of ideas scratched on old notepads. Alida Brill brought her sharp theatrical intelligence to help me untie some difficult literary knots, and Patsy Rodenburg from London loudly pushed me forward and demanded that I keep on.

I give my thanks to Deborah Kampmeier, and to many other actors and students for supporting me and reminding me of elements of my teaching which they found central to their work—Mary Beth Peil, Laurie Kennedy, Boyd Gaines, James Karen, Diana Douglas—many of these actors read early versions and urged me forward.

Two people have been very important to my work. First is Allen McCullough, that good actor, who has stage managed and recorded my class for many years. Then there is my overall assistant for all things, in all matters of my life, the good Bridget St. John, who stepped in numberless times to lend a hand and who is, at this very moment, taking this dictation. Thank you, Bridget.

Ten years ago, I sold the Michael Howard Studios, its name, its history, its lease, a piano, and some chairs to Gabrielle Berberich and her partners. Selling the studio assured me the space to continue my work and the time for the writing of this book, and for that, I am grateful. I thank them for honoring the vision I laid out for Michael Howard Studios as they continue to move the studio forward.

I could go on with this list, name after name, of all the actors who in some particular way shared my work life. Such a list would include actor-teachers who took copious notes in a given class, went home and typed them up, then came back and said: "Here, this is important. Do a book, Michael." Alex Neil did it. The late, sorely missed Gloria Maddox did it.

Mark Lewis, a man of extraordinary empathy and insight (and "outsight," if there is such) is first among many acting teachers— actors all—who may not know they are very specifically part of this book, but because they generously shared my ideas with their students, have helped me see my own work more clearly. Here are some of them: Michael Kahn, Richard Warner, Terry Schreiber, Peter Lobdell, Judith Levitt, David Landon, Leslie Jacobson, Judy Lee Vivier, and Michael Bofshever.

Lastly, a sweet and gentle thank you to all the actors who, over the past sixty-five years, have helped me better understand what it means to say . . . "I am an Actor."

Index